Chris Joseph walked out of university to become a priest. It was a tough decision, and the tasks set by the bishop, even tougher. From nightclub bouncer to Benedictine monk, he worked in a dilapidated iron foundry where he survived a horrific industrial accident. Disabled but undaunted, he finished his degree before joining the world of advertising. Having established his own award-winning agency in the heart of London's west end, he was struck down by mental illness and the inevitable stigma and chaos that accompany instability. He used his advertising skills to publicise and settle High Court copyright and banking disputes with several high profile multinational companies including Barclays Bank.

'Manicdotes-there's madness in his method' is a series of short true humorous and horrific stories from Chris Joseph's life that can be read together or in isolation. They should give readers an insight into the joyful, painful, but certainly crazy world that he has inhabited where insanity often follows creativity. Whether its madness or genius you be the judge...!

MANICDOTES – THERE'S
MADNESS IN HIS METHOD

CHRIS JOSEPH

MANICDOTES – THERE'S
MADNESS IN HIS METHOD

AUSTIN MACAULEY

A CIP catalogue record for this title is available from the British Library.

ISBN 978 1 905609 07-9

www.austinmacauley.com

First Published (2008)
Austin & Macauley Publishers Ltd.
25 Canada Square
Canary Wharf
London
E14 5LB

Printed & Bound in Great Britain

DEDICATION

To my children, Caitlin, Rebecca and Leo

My sincere apologies to anyone I have forgotten or offended –
there's no 'arm intended

ACKNOWLEDGEMENTS

My thanks to my family and friends, who have willingly picked up the pieces when my life has fallen apart. Thanks also to the people who have directly or indirectly contributed to this book by their actions, whether good or bad towards me, for enriching my life and experience. No pain, no gain.

Also Nigel Spaven my graphic artist, John Tylee, Associate Editor of Campaign Magazine for writing the foreword, photographer Steve Gale, Mike Kulezich for the George Best photograph, members of SAFE, Geoff Hobson, Bob Gaught and Keith Whincup, who also provided photographs, the Middlesbrough Evening Gazette for photographs.

FOREWORD

I first met Chris Joseph as the result of a press release faxed (yes, it was that long ago) to the newsdesk at Campaign magazine. I still have it. The words are so faded as to be barely legible but the note scrawled across the top of it from Campaign's news editor is still distinguishable. "Do you know this man?" she asked. "Could you call him and check out this story?"

Following up leads of this kind was a regular part of my job. The weekly magazine was often dubbed the "Bible" of the advertising industry, reporting on the highs and lows of the colourful characters who provided its collective vitality and creative potency.

Unlike many other Campaign journalists at the time, I'd cut my teeth in newspapers. Court reporting and stories involving legal disputes were familiar to me. When such stories emerged at Campaign, they tended to be pushed my way.

And what an intriguing story Chris Joseph had to tell. In short, the then boss of a small Soho advertising agency had slapped a £1 million lawsuit on four major international companies – Barclays, Philips, Shell and Hutchison Telecommunications. His allegations were truly incendiary – that rights to a logo he had designed to spearhead a multimillion pound campaign to launch the Rabbit mobile phone system had been illegally taken from him and that there had been a conspiracy to put him out of business.

My first reaction was that I was about to phone a man either very brave or very stupid. If he was really intent on doing what he said, then he was going where no other adman had dared go before. Ad agencies invariably shied away from suing clients for fear other business prospects would shun them. They bit the bullet. And that had sometimes allowed clients to get away with murder. Here suddenly was somebody prepared to stand up to powerful business interests and seemingly risk financial ruin in the process.

Reading a little of what had already been written about him only reinforced my concern that this was somebody who revelled in his own self-publicity. The ad industry, by its nature, has always attracted such types. I was once sent a Christmas card by an outrageously camp creative director that featured himself lying naked on a sheepskin rug, his modesty protected only by strategically placed bottle of Bollinger!

Chris, it appeared, could hold his own even when judged against these flamboyant standards. He had once towed a mobile billboard to the headquarters of Barclays demanding compensation for an alleged four-month delay in settling a £737,000 bill. On another occasion, having had problems with a faulty car, he placed a billboard listing the faults opposite the dealer's showroom. He got his money back.

What's more, his swashbuckling approach to perceived injustices seemed to be symbolised by the solid silver hook replacing the right arm that had been ripped off in an horrific industrial accident several years earlier. He'd even called his agency Hook Advertising.

The fact that he'd once been a novice Benedictine monk, a would-be Catholic priest and a nightclub bouncer only made an already extraordinary story truly bizarre. As I was to discover over the next few years when Chris was battling his personal demons, it was also a dark and poignant one.

His manic depression has dragged him to the edge of the precipice and habitually threatened to push him over. His often troubled mind is also sharp and questioning. Early struggles with officialdom to win increases in paltry disability allowances have bred a dogged determination to see justice done. And by drawing on his skills as an advertising and marketing man ("I know how to make it simple and get people to relate to it"), he has proved that the little person who finds themselves mistreated by a giant corporation need not just roll over; that all such companies have vulnerable spot if only you can find it.

Sounds simple? Far from it. Taking on one of these behemoths needs courage, tenacity and resourcefulness. You must learn how to use the law when possible, devise publicity to shame and embarrass your adversaries when it isn't.

What's more, you must live with the knowledge that, should you fail, you may end up penniless. The strain on your health and your family relationships may become unendurable. In Chris's case, his perseverance has its roots in the life-changing experience that his accident brought about. As he puts it: "When you've looked death in the face nothing can be as frightening."

Small wonder that he has lived a large part of his life on an emotional rollercoaster fuelled by his illness. The chemical imbalance in his brain can result in alarmingly obsessional behaviour. He once trashed a room in a desperate search to find a solution to a problem that was plaguing him.

His moods could swing between the elation of winning yet another legal skirmish to the obsessive. Trying to get him off the phone on a busy press day as he explained his latest wheeze to humble one of his adversaries wasn't easy. "Chris has a passionate belief in what he's doing and bags of enthusiasm," one of his long-time friends once told me. "The downside is that he's never learned humility."

Worst of all, though, were the rambling calls from somebody clearly hyped up and about to crack up. And I'll not quickly forget the heavily drugged. unkempt and unshaven figure shuffling through the corridors of London's High Court to pursue his last case having been rescued from a mental institution in Morocco. He had fled to North Africa, he later explained to me, to satisfy his sudden desire to explore and meet new people, toss away the hook that had become his trademark and exorcise the terrible memories associated with it.

Now, Chris has chosen to take his personal exorcism a stage further by telling his story. It will make you laugh. It will move you. By the end of it, you may well marvel that he is still around to write it given all that life has thrown at him.

I'd like to be able to tell you that it has a happy ending. But reality isn't like that. There's the comfort of knowing that Chris has exchanged the adrenalin-charged life for a quieter existence back home in North-East England. He's learned to control his illness by regular medication and not to take on the kind of frenzied activity that could trigger a relapse.

15

He never got the multi-million pound legal settlement that many thought was his entitlement. Nor could a marriage that produced three children survive the relentless strain that he put upon it.

The best that can be said is that Chris is at peace with himself. It's about as close to humility as he's ever likely to get.

John Tylee
Associate Editor of Campaign magazine

CHAPTER 1

Introduction

It was a couple of days after September 11th 2001, just after the twin towers had been demolished in New York. It was the end of the world, the money markets would collapse, and World War III was about to break-out or at least that's what I believed. I also believed that I could, and would, save the world. I was hypermanic. I had made a beeline from the North-east to London and had just attended a meeting with various dignitaries at the House of Lords accompanied by David Shayler, the former MI5 officer turned "whistleblower", and my young assistant, Greg. We were all smartly dressed in suits and popped into the Il Sorriso restaurant on Charlotte Street, opposite Saatchi & Saatchi Advertising, for an Italian meal. There was no expense spared and I willingly paid the bill. Then we walked towards Soho and disappeared into a members-only gentlemen's club under Goodge Street that was full of prostitutes, all touting for business in the smoky, perfume-laden air. I politely refused to pay for a lady for each of my companions and we made our way to Soho where we ended up drinking champagne with the lap dancers in Peter Stringfellow's nightclub until the early hours of the morning. We made our way back to home base in Kent and I immediately ordered a "take-a-way". That is my affectionate term for an escort girl. She cost me £500 in cash. She was enjoying herself, flaunting herself in the mirrors that covered the bedroom walls of my mate Geoff's house – she was convinced she was being filmed. It was great fun.

Three weeks later I was back in the North-east in the secure unit of a psychiatric hospital with seven members of staff pinning me to the ground as another injected me in the rear with enough of a drug that was sufficient to knock out a horse. This was, needless to say, no fun at all. From Messiah to pariah in the space of a few days – this has been my burden for nearly twenty years. Here's how it all began.

Chapter 2

Opting In

My story does not really begin until I walked out of the University of Liverpool at the end of my first year of my B.A. Honours degree at the age of 19 in 1977. I was driven by what I can only describe as an awakening of my social conscience. Away from the safe environment of our home in Teesside, I had woken up to a realisation that there was so much suffering around me and throughout the world that I felt that even if I could alleviate it slightly then I would be making a difference. I suddenly realised that the only reason I was doing a French degree was because I was good at languages. I had studied Latin, Greek, French and Russian at school and had come out with twelve O Levels and three A Levels. I had passed the Oxford University entrance exam but had failed on interview, so I had opted for a red brick university, where I would pursue my aptitude for French and where I could indulge in my passion for watching football. Then it all suddenly dawned on me. I was in a rut. My whole life appeared to be mapped out in front of me; I would probably end up a diplomat or a French teacher and I would retire at sixty-five and be given a gold watch or a greenhouse for my years of service. Then, having done nothing to 'make a difference', I would anonymously fade away. While at university I had had a chance to reflect on my Roman Catholic upbringing. I was born of parents who had come over to England from India and settled during the early fifties. My heritage came from a mixture of an Anglo-Indian father called Basil and an Indo-Portuguese mother called Marie. My ancestors on my father's side were also of Portuguese descent. My father was from the North of India – a Chief Engineer in the Indian merchant navy, and my mother was an English teacher in Bombay. Having taken virtually any engineering job he could when he first arrived in the UK, my father raised the money for her fare and sent for my mother to come to Britain. He eventually ended up as the Standards Engineer for Imperial Chemical Industries (ICI) in Teesside and my mother taught English to Advanced level in a number of schools in the North-east. My siblings and I were born in England and the only language we spoke at home was English.

My childhood had been a happy one; one spent fishing and shooting with my father and playing the piano and clarinet with my brother and sister. My mother was an excellent cook and my parents always made sure we were well fed and well protected. We went on many family holidays to the south of Ireland and up to Scotland. I have always been a fanatical supporter of Middlesbrough Football Club and when, in my teens I followed them round the country. It was an expensive hobby, but we managed to fund ourselves by winning a competition in the local sports paper that paid out a crisp five pound note every week. My good friend, George O'Neill, and I won that competition some seventeen times in all. It was a simple matter of spotting the differences between two drawings and filling out a witty caption or tagline. When we realised that the editors of the local newspaper would not allow the competition to be won by the same people on consecutive weeks; we used other identities, giving a cut of our winnings to our friends, some of whom were satisfied with just the kudos of seeing their names in the paper as winners. On one occasion, we filled in the competition entry in the guise and childlike writing of a seven-year-old girl who was clearly getting help from her dad. We won the money and she was delighted to see her name in print in the paper the following week. I suppose that this competition was where I first made money from my creative and copywriting skills.

My parents were fervent Roman Catholics and we only attended Catholic schools. My sister, Vanessa, who is a year older than me and my brother Tim, who is a year younger, are both still practising Roman Catholics. We spent many years of our very happy, but sheltered, childhood as a family group, ritually chanting responses to the Rosary at home or at Mass, not only on a Sunday but whenever we could. My faith was very strong and very blind; the natural progression for me to fulfil my vocation was to see if I could join the Roman Catholic priesthood. Having visited all my close friends to inform them of my decision, I returned to Teesside to put in my application to Ushaw College, a priest training college in Durham. My parents were shocked but, needless to say, delighted.

In those days of declining numbers of vocations to the priesthood, I would be welcomed with open arms. It was still hard to pass the various interviews you had to go through to join the priest training college at the time. As I recall, my various interviews took place on the day Scotland last beat England at the old Wembley Stadium and invaded the pitch and stole the goalposts and half the turf! I reluctantly ended up missing the match. I remember having two very rigorous interviews and perhaps the most intrusive medical examination I have ever had to endure. Believe me, absolutely everything was checked because in Canon law (the law of the Church) at the time, you had to be a "complete" man to become a priest. I believe that even these days a dispensation has to be granted if you are incomplete in any way, although this particular law may have been relaxed. Historically this was because during the Middle Ages, the mentally and physically impaired sons of the aristocracy were regularly sent into the bosom of the Church to join the priesthood. During solemn worship, their speech impediments, tics, and infirmities would cause much merriment amongst the congregation, so a law was introduced to remove these would-be priests before they were ordained. Then came the main interview. It was with the Bishop and twelve priests; six older and six younger. The Bishop of Hexham and Newcastle at the time was Hugh Lindsay. He asked me the killer question: What did I think about celibacy? I answered honestly that I thought celibacy was "unnatural". There was a muttering from the priests around the table; the younger ones nodded their assent, the older ones their disapproval. The rest of the interview was fine. I was asked to leave the room and returned a few minutes later to be told that my application had been unsuccessful for that year. The Bishop informed me that he was going to send me out for a year to undertake various tasks and to get more experience of life, especially the more spiritual side of the vocation. He said that if I still wanted to join the seminary the following year, I would be most welcome. My local parish priests, Frs. John O'Gorman and Brian Murphy, were to act as mentors and assist me if I needed any guidance.

CHAPTER 3

The "Fiesta"

Although my parents were delighted to have me back at home, I decided to get myself a job. Across the road from our home was the most fabulous cabaret nightclub. It was called the "Fiesta" and was twinned with another Fiesta in Sheffield run by the same family. It attracted all the major artists and cabaret stars of the time and was the place for the 'beautiful people' to be seen and enjoy themselves. People from all over the region and beyond travelled miles for a night out at the Fiesta. The guests were always very smartly dressed and came from all age groups. I had worked briefly as a barman during the summer and, to the absolute horror of my parents, I persuaded the manager of the Fiesta to employ me; not as a barman but as a doorman. The club had numerous bars and a casino, and my parents, who had never gone to a nightclub, were convinced that I had taken a job in Sodom or Gomorrah. I had persuaded the management that I could use brains rather than brawn to deal with the flashpoints that occurred in the club. I was, in truth, uncertain whether I could keep my nerve but I was tested on the third night of my arrival. Decked out in my tuxedo and bow tie, I had been allocated the job of Floor Manager, and as such had to arrange the seating plans for the arena. I also had to take requests from the guests for the compere to read out. Thursday night is the traditional night for stag and hen parties and I had arranged my floor plan to keep various male parties apart and mix them with female tables. But while I was taking the requests behind the stage to the compere, one of my fellow doormen unwittingly seated a group of 40 lads from Newcastle beside another 40 from Middlesbrough. The cabaret that evening was called "Sweet Sensation". Half way into their act, the Boro lads realised they were sitting next to the Geordies. Football chants of "Middlesbro'" followed by chants of "Newcastle" rose above the music. Then there was an almighty punch-up down one side of the club. The rivals smashed chairs, bottles, glasses and table lights over each others' heads. The cabaret carried on singing and the shutters came down on the bar adjacent to the fight. We had seven bouncers working that evening including me. The head doorman told us not to intervene until they had worn each other out. We waited, called the police, and then went in and calmed everyone down. I felt something hit the back of my head. It was a glass. I rounded on the man who had glassed me and asked him for an explanation. Although my adrenalin was pumping, I made no attempt to hit him back. He was so taken aback that I had not retaliated that he turned sheepishly away and stopped fighting. After that evening, I knew I could keep my nerve.

CHAPTER 4

The Arab's Trousers

As I was polite to the customers and would happily engage them in conversation, I was very quickly moved to front the main door. Although I had a team of doormen behind me in the reception, I would meet and greet the customers and decide whether they were too drunk to come in or perhaps did not meet the strict smart dress code. This involved tact and diplomacy combined with a degree of firmness. On one occasion a dark-skinned man in his twenties approached the door. I told him that he could not come in because he was wearing jeans. He informed me that he was an Arab prince who was doing an engineering degree at Sunderland Polytechnic and complained that he was smartly dressed apart from his jeans, and had travelled a long way to come to the club that evening. I refused him entry again and he initially started to get abusive. Suddenly, from behind him, appeared a very large man who confronted me. "Perhaps this will help" he said, and introduced himself as the Arab's bodyguard. He was holding out a crisp new £50 note. Believe me, that was a lot of money in those days. "You know what you can do with your money?" I replied. "What exactly?" he retorted, whilst raising himself up to his full height and squaring up to me. I pointed to the bus stop a few yards away. "There's a man at that bus stop. Go and swap your jeans for his trousers and give him the fifty quid. He looks the same size as you." A couple of minutes later the Arab and his minder returned to the steps of the Fiesta. The trousers fitted perfectly. The man at the bus stop was delighted, and I had no problem letting them in.

CHAPTER 5

The Iron Fist

One evening at the Fiesta I was summoned to a fight that had broken out on the stage. Apparently a man had punched his girlfriend on the dance floor because she had danced with another man. The two men were at each other's throats. When I got to the scene there was only one other doorman. His name was Roger. We grappled with the man who had started the fight and escorted him down a corridor leading to a fire exit. Despite the fact that we had both his arms pulled up behind his back, he was struggling furiously with us. He was clearly very drunk and I know that he was convinced that we were going to beat him up outside the club. We just wanted to put him out and tell him not to come back. When we got to the fire exit, I realised to my horror, that the metal bar across the exit had not been removed for the evening. I held on to the drunk while Roger struggled with the iron bar. Then Roger made a cardinal error. He let go of one of his arms and the drunk grabbed my left hand. Before I could pull it away he snapped the fourth and fifth digits on my left hand like twigs, pulling them back over my hand in the opposite direction to their natural position. He laughed out loud. He knew exactly what he was doing. Priest or no priest, I could not help myself. I waved my mangled hand to distract him and simultaneously kicked him in the groin. As he bent double, I punched him full on the jaw with my right fist. He keeled over unconscious. Then the head doorman Kenny arrived. We had become good friends and he was very angry that my fingers had been broken. Before I could intervene, he yanked the man's arm up behind his back until we heard it crack. I was sickened by Kenny's actions but he insisted that the man had to be taught a lesson. I went to the hospital and my fingers were manipulated and strapped up.

The police had been called to the hospital because the man had arrived there and wanted to press charges against me for his broken arm. In the event, he took the matter no further. The following morning my parents were horrified. They did not want me to return to the club but I was adamant. I went back with my hand strapped up and, for added protection; I wore a black leather glove on the injured hand. Every day I strengthened the fingers by playing the piano. Word got quickly around that you did not mess with the dark-skinned doorman (me!); not only was he a black belt in karate but he had a false iron fist in his black glove. I did nothing to dispel the rumours as they worked in my favour. Little did I realise the irony of that period of healing where I learned to do many things one-handed through necessity.

CHAPTER 6

From Bouncer To Monk

I really enjoyed my days as a bouncer at the Fiesta. The atmosphere was electric and the women were gorgeous. I wasn't a priest yet so I was in my element. It was like being in a candy shop. The last thing on my mind was the priesthood. But I was in for an almighty shock. I received instructions from the Bishop that I should go immediately to join a monastery in Scotland. Founded in 1230AD by King Alexander II, Pluscarden Abbey is the only medieval monastery in Scotland still occupied by monks, and it is a place of worship, work and reflection. Pluscarden is a silent order Benedictine monastery near to Elgin in Morayshire. The Bishop and my mentors had decided it was time to move me on from, what they considered to be, a very worldly environment and I was to join the noviciate in this monastery and experience the more spiritual side of my Faith. Before I knew it, I was on a train heading north. What a culture shock it was; to be enjoying the glamour and glitz of the nightclub one Tuesday night and then to find yourself in the cloisters of a huge old building and in the company of a strange looking group of skinheads the following Friday! The first thing I saw as I entered the main door was a young man with his head closely shaven swinging on the rope of a tolling bell. The monastery was austere, set on its own in countryside, a few miles away from Perth. The buildings were made of grey stone. There was very little in the form of decoration, except in the church, that was attached to the building. The grounds outside were beautiful and deer would stray in every now and then from the wooded hillside, so tranquil was the setting. The habit of a Benedictine monk is usually black but the monks of Pluscarden wear a white habit made of wool, having been granted a special dispensation to do so. We novices wore grey habits with a handy cowl, so you could hide from snap-happy tourists when they came to visit or stay. While I was at Pluscarden I worked in the laundry with Brother Bede, so you might say that I cleaned up the monks' dirty habits. I also worked in the fields, as the monastery farmed its own land and was largely self-sufficient at the time, using barter to trade with the local community where it was lacking. The Abbot at the time kept bees and the monks sold the honey and their produce in their tourists' gift shop. We would get up at the crack of dawn to go to the chapel and sing matins and lauds in Gregorian Latin chant and would celebrate Mass, evensong and vespers as the day went by. There were some fifty monks with five members of the noviciate. I found my own knowledge of Latin to be particularly useful whilst in the monastery, as I could understand the psalms we were singing but I was disturbed by the given notion that the brothers, who did not necessarily even understand what they were singing about, were nevertheless devoting themselves to praising God. The food was spectacularly good as the cook was a Brother Joseph, who had previously been a chef at the Gleneagles Hotel. Yes, without doubt, meals were the best moments of the day for me. However, meals, as indeed was the case with every other activity, were governed by the "Lesser" and the "Greater" silences (the first where you were allowed to communicate if necessary, and the other, total silence). With our healthy appetites from working in the fields and with the wonderfully clean air, following grace there would be a feeding frenzy while a monk would read from the pulpit in the dining area. I have never really been able to slow myself down in eating a meal since I spent time in Pluscarden. The monks were generous towards me, answering my never-ending chatter of questions during the Lesser Silence so that they did not break their vows of silence. I worked in the kitchen with Brother Joseph and picked up a few culinary skills along the way. I also learned about making stained glass windows from Brother Anselm and pig farming from Brother Giles who was a giant of a man. As novices, we were cut off from the outside world and not even allowed to read a newspaper. There was no television or radio. I surprised the Novice Master one morning when he said that the news was full of the death of a pop star and I immediately piped up with Marc Bolan's name. I had heard it on a portable radio that I had brought to the monastery, and which the monks thought was a compass due to its round dial. I was told in the nicest possible way not to use the radio. On another occasion, I was caught having stolen into the older monks, common room to get the result of the Middlesbrough v Sunderland local football derby from the newspapers. I was severely admonished when I explained what I was doing there, but the "Boro" had won 1-0 so I didn't care. My bouncer friends in the nightclub stayed in touch with me by mail and raised my hopes and spirits, as I did my time, by promising to mount a raid to get me out to see a group of sexy female artistes who were ex-Page Three girls and had formed a singing group. The break-out from the monastery, needless to say, never occurred.

CHAPTER 7

Rude Awakening

Each morning, the monks would get up at 5am for matins. One week I was selected to wake early (4.30am) and knock on the doors of the monks' cells to wake them for matins. I had to steal around the eerie dark corridors of the monastery, knocking on each door and saying the words "Benedicamus domino" which translates as "Let us bless the Lord". The sleeping monk would wake and reply "Et cum spirito tuo" – "And may the Holy Spirit be with you" – or more often than not grunt something inaudible and sometimes profane and I would move on to the next cell. As I stumbled along in the blackness, holding my candle, I spotted something in the furthest reaches of the corridor. It was flying at head height towards me as if in slow motion. I had seen the Hammer horror films. It must be a vampire bat! As it approached, I pulled my cowl up over my head and ducked to avoid it. I must have thrown out its natural radar. It flew straight into my hood and landed squarely on my head. I let out an enormous yell. I must have been loud. All the monks woke up in unison and various brothers, dressed in their pyjamas, came rushing to my aid. I was struggling with the creature in my hood. I was most embarrassed when I found out it was not a monster from my childhood nightmares, but merely a particularly large but harmless bat of which there were thousands that lived in the area surrounding the monastery. What a wuss!

Chapter 8

Day Off

My time in the monastery happened to coincide with the monks' annual holiday. It was a summer's day and the weather was beautiful. On this day the monks were all transported to a beautiful secluded cove, with its own sandy beach. The gathered troupe of monks were allowed to dress in mufti for the day off and it was a bizarre sight indeed, as we travelled along the windy roads to the beach on a large trailer pulled by a tractor. The older monks were taken there in a minibus. The monks were all of different ages, having joined the monastery over the years and at different times in their lives. Therefore their clothes came from different eras, with some very old monks in garb from the twenties or even earlier and others with fashions leading all the way up to the seventies. It looked like a posh tramps' day out. When we got to the beach, we were allowed to talk freely and play football or simply climb up the hill to reflect and enjoy the serenity of the cove and the sea air. Some brothers chose to smoke cigarettes and we had dark chocolate and, to my delight, Newcastle Brown Ale. Brother Giles, who was a very large man, stripped down to his swimming trunks and swam right out to the horizon of the cove. He could be seen all day, swimming between the two cliffs like the shark in the movie "Jaws". Whenever you cast your eye to the horizon, there he would be heading from left to right or vice versa. He only came in to eat a couple of sandwiches and then returned to the sea for the rest of the day. I enjoyed myself playing football, eating Brother Joseph's delicious food and, of course, drinking the Brown Ale.

Chapter 9

Painkiller

Having travelled both to and from the beach on the back of the open trailer, that night I suffered the most dreadful rheumatic pain in my back. I could not and did not sleep all night and was not looking forward to getting back to the drill in the early morning. At 5 am I was in terrible pain and knocked on the door of the novice head, Fr. Maurus. I told him of my pain and he told me to go back to my cell and wait for him. He got dressed and came to my room. He put a pillow on the floor and covered me with a blanket. Then he advised me to concentrate on the toes on my right foot. He wanted me to shut off any sensation in my toes. He then told me to concentrate on my foot, and then my ankle, and then my other foot. Slowly, but surely, I concentrated and shut down the different parts of my body until I found myself in a very deep state of relaxation and eventually, a sound sleep. I slept all day on the hard wooden floorboards and was eventually awakened by a monk who brought me chicken broth to my room with some of Br. Joseph's homemade bread. I was completely refreshed and the pain was gone. Throughout my life I have been able to draw on Fr. Maurus's method to relieve pain. It was to stand me in good stead in the future.

I left the monastery on good terms. When deciding whether a trainee can be accepted to join the monastery, the monks operate a black balling system. They have a secret ballot where, if any one of them votes against you, you will be rejected from the monastery. They had a ballot for me and told me they had unanimously agreed they would welcome me to join the brethren. But a life of reflection was not for me. I felt – and still do – that the monks were wasting their obvious talents and skills by opting out of the real world. They would argue that they had opted in to praising God. The brief period of reflection and spiritualism had also given me an insight into what would be required of me if I were to join the priesthood. I left after a few months and came back to the North-east of England.

CHAPTER 10

The Iron Foundry

It was still my intention to join the seminary but before that, I resolved to get myself a manual job in heavy industry. The Bishop and my mentors had no objection and regarded my intentions as all good experience. I have always approached different business enterprises by turning up and insisting on an interview with the managing director. Getting a job was no different. I turned up one morning at Head Wrightson Iron Cast on the outskirts of Stockton-on-Tees. I clearly impressed, as the managing director told me to start work as a maintenance fitter's mate the next day. The iron foundry was certainly the filthiest place I have ever worked in. The air was full of thick, black smoke that bellowed from the two huge working tilting furnaces and the air in the casting shop was a mixture of black dust, sand and resin, with the pungent stink of acid mixed in. This was the concoction used to make the moulds for casting the produce of the foundry. The moulds were then broken up and recycled to make new ones. It was a very dirty process. We were making cast iron segments for rings to be used in tunnels. Imagine a rectangle standing on its longer side and then curved into a segment like in an orange. Bolt seven of these huge segments together, and you had a ring. Bolt the rings together and you get a tunnel. The contract we were working on at that time was to send segments for tunnels in Argentina. I loved the work. It made me very strong. We were required virtually twenty-four hours a day to maintain the foundry. I later discovered that this was because every time the foundry had been closed down between contracts, it had not been put into "mothballs" – this was a process by which a maintenance team would be employed to keep the plant ticking over and updating and renovating the machinery where necessary.

Instead, whenever the foundry got a contract, a small team of fitters and electricians were employed just to get the machines up and running again. Therefore, the machinery was often out of date and decaying and up to date improvements in safety were simply overlooked in the hasty efforts to get the foundry working again as soon as possible. Also in that foundry, the management chose to cannibalise old machinery, such as cranes, to replace spare parts, rather than ordering and fitting new ones. This may have saved time and money, but it added to the dangerous environment. I got on famously with my new workmates and very quickly became known throughout the plant as I worked with my fitter "Eric" and the rest of the team. We were regularly scaling giant sand hoppers, both outside and inside the plant, and replacing large valves and joints in pipes. We carried substantial tools and equipment, including huge sledgehammers and massive spanners, onto different maintenance jobs and repaired the giant overhead travelling cranes that traversed the foundry bay and the casting shop. It was very heavy but rewarding work. I was extremely fit and became very powerfully built. But never once in the six months I was there did anyone talk about safety. The foundry had a safety officer and a medical officer. The safety officer had an injured leg from a previous industrial accident and wore a business suit and never climbed onto any of the machinery. I was to find out later that many safety officers had suffered industrial accidents and were later offered safety management roles as a way of appeasing them. Then I tried to join the union; but the shop steward would not accept me arguing that I was a student thereby keeping a union man out of a job. On my day off, I went to the local branch of the TGWU (Transport and General Workers Union) and joined there. They were pleased to sign me up.

CHAPTER 11

Near Misses

Looking back at my brief days in the foundry, there were too many instances to recall where my life was in danger. There are three that spring readily to mind. As I said, the tunnel segments were made of cast iron and from moulds that were made of sand, acid and resin. When these moulds were recycled, they were broken up on a moving iron machine called a "shake out" and the resulting crushed black powder and dust were transferred back to the huge sand hoppers outside the casting shop for reuse. There was a gigantic extractor-fan at the end of the casting bay and this would suck out the thick black dust in the air and deposit it in a water tank that was the size of a large juggernaut. Then blades, at two feet intervals on chains, would scoop the residue out and deposit it in skips that were periodically removed and emptied. The machine was called a "wet arrestor". That was the theory. In practice, this machine would constantly be allowed to choke up and as we were the maintenance team we would be sent inside the wet arrestor to flush it out with hosepipes. One freezing night in January, I was inside the wet arrestor with another man from the maintenance squad. We were clad in waterproof suits with masks and were busy blasting and shifting the black and hardened silt and ice that had choked up the machine with our high-pressure hoses. Suddenly, the machine groaned and creaked and sprang into action. Both my companion and I, fortunately, reacted immediately. We jumped up and placed our feet into the grooves above and on both sides of the blades and, straddling the moving chains, pulled ourselves out of the machine by holding onto the hosepipes and using them as ropes. The electricians had not isolated the machine. They had forgotten to switch off the power and had returned to the warmth of the maintenance shop for a cup of tea. I complained to the safety officer about the incident. No action was taken – indeed I don't think the incident was ever even logged.

On another occasion, I had been called to clear up an oil spillage under one of the iron furnaces. These were not blast furnaces but gigantic electric coil furnaces. They would be powered up and "charged" with scrap metal from overhead travelling cranes operated by crane drivers, who travelled backwards and forwards some fifty feet above the furnace bay lowering and raising huge electromagnets and dropping scrap iron into the gaping hot furnaces. When the metal was molten and ready to pour, the crane drivers would transfer metal containers lined with tiles and affectionately known as "teapots" and the furnaces would raise up on massive hydraulic ramps and tilt the iron into the teapots to be transferred to the casting shop. What has never ceased to amaze me about working in that foundry was the sheer scale of the operation and the tasks undertaken there. To see hot metal being poured and made on a television screen bears no comparison to actually seeing it taking place. The heat and the light alone are awesome. Both furnaces were switched off and it had been decided to carry out routine maintenance on them while they were "down". However, there had been a large spillage of hydraulic oil under one of the furnaces and it needed to be cleaned up, as it was potentially a fire risk. I went onto the top of the furnace to tell the no.1 furnace operator that I was going under the furnace. I was equipped with several buckets of sawdust, a shovel and a brush. I unlocked the door under the furnace, went in and set about my task. I had been inside for about a half hour when, to my horror, there was a loud humming sound just above my head. I realised in an instant what it was. It was the sound of the "buzz" bars coming alive. These are the metal bars that carry the voltage necessary to charge up the coils to heat up the furnace. It is because they carry so much power that they cannot be insulated and to have touched one with my brush or shovel would have meant instant electrocution. I got out of there very quickly indeed and went onto the furnace to remonstrate with the foreman. He had disappeared for a while and, in his absence, the second in command had started up the furnaces. They had completely forgotten that I was under there. I reported the incident to my superior but he took it no further for fear of rocking the boat.

As I had demonstrated my ability to learn quickly and take the initiative, one day the managing director took me aside and told me he would like to promote me to "Lubrications Engineer". This is the posh name for a "greaser" and he increased my paltry wage by 50p per hour. Little did I know that I was taking on the most dangerous job in the foundry because, in this workplace, production did not stop for maintenance. There was no training given to me for the role of greaser. I was supposed to ask the maintenance team what tools, grease guns, and oils or grease to use, but they had neither the time, nor the knowledge to take time from their own busy schedules to explain what was necessary. One day I was called to top up the oil on the shot blaster. This is a machine the size of a terraced house. The cast-iron tunnel segments were transported by the overhead cranes and locked inside the huge blue metal doors of the shot blaster. Once inside, the segment is bombarded with steel ball-bearings and the rough edges are effectively removed, so that it can go to the next part of the process which is "fettling" where the excess metal is ground off the segment before it is finished by machining. Having climbed up the ladder and installed myself on the top of the shot blast, I started to add the lubricants to the machine. The machine suddenly sprang into life. The shot blast, like many of the machines in the foundry, was a machine that, in operating itself, would systematically erode itself from within. The ball-bearings hurtled around with such force inside the machine, that eventually they wore holes in its ever-thinning walls. The metal plated walls were constantly being replaced, much to the annoyance of the management. I was on top of the machine being peppered with steel ball-bearings. I covered my eyes, curled into a ball and waited for the machine to finish its cycle. Then I clambered down and screamed at the operator. He said he'd forgotten I was there. This was once again a machine that should have been isolated before maintenance but with no safety procedures or training given, and workers not wanting to drop others in it, it was the blind leading the blind.

Chapter 12

Industrial Accident

I was leading a charmed life and had plenty of time to think about my vocation as I innocently went on with my manual labour. I had worked in the foundry for some six months before I reached the conclusion that I could not, in all sincerity, enter the seminary when I did not agree with one of the Roman Catholic Church's fundamental rules – that of celibacy. I remember that it took more courage to tell my parents and others that I had changed my mind, than it did to tell them I was going to be a priest in the first place. I recall that my two mentors visited my parents' house and we all prayed together in acceptance of my decision and for guidance. That night, with a massive weight off my mind, I put on my best light grey flannel suit, and went over the road to the Fiesta nightclub to see my friends. I had not been in the nightclub for many months and I was welcomed back with open arms. I did not have a drink, or stay for long, as I had work in the morning.

On May 24th 1978, I climbed into my mustard-coloured Mini Cooper and drove to work as usual. I put on my overalls, safety helmet and boots and headed for the maintenance shop. As ever, there was a group of my mates milling around drinking pints of tea and coffee. It was a beautiful sunny day outside. I had hardly sat down when a worker from the casting shop came in and told me that there was an urgent job to do on one of the massive overhead travelling cranes. He said that the main gears (cogs) on the hoist on the crane had seized up, and were groaning and needed greasing. I had never greased the open gears on a hoist before, so I asked if someone would come with me. However, everyone was busy having their tea, so I ended up going on my own. I grabbed two tubes of grease and my grease gun and put on my industrial gloves. I entered the casting shop and with the tubes of grease tucked firmly in my belt and climbed up the metal ladders to the walkway along the edge of the shop. The driver was below me in the cab, suspended under the crane. I climbed onto the hoist and lifted the plate metal lid to the gearbox. I was looking into a square hole and could see two giant cogs meshing with each other, like you may see in a watch. These were the most prodigious cogs on the crane, as they had to deal with the actual loads of cast iron themselves. I squirted in the first tube of thick grey grease and climbed down to tell the crane driver to slowly hoist up the huge electromagnet. I was not prepared for what followed. The whole crane shuddered as the gears cranked into motion and I fell forward. I put my right hand out to stop myself and the second tube went right between the gears. Try as I might, I could not let go of it. Before I knew it, the cogs had seized the gloved fingers on my right hand and they were slowly disappearing into the gearbox. To this day, I can vividly recall my fingers snapping as they were slowly but surely crushed. The horror of what was happening suddenly hit me. I could only watch as the rest of my hand crept inexorably between the gears and then the gears grasped the sleeve of my overall. I felt phenomenal pain, and it dawned on me that the mouth of the gearbox was large enough for me to fit through and I was going to be pulled right into the gearbox and would surely die. I frantically reached for the shifting spanner that I always carried with me to ram it between the gears, but it lay beside me on the gantry and I was being pulled away from it. I remember that it took a while for me to register what was going on. I was about to be eaten alive by a massive mincing machine. Then I let out an almighty scream. It was all I could do to save myself. It was a death scream, a scream that you issue with every fibre in your body; it comes from your very soul. That scream was heard in every part of the iron foundry except for the crane driver and in a flash, a man on the shop floor waved his arms to the crane driver to stop the crane immediately. When the first man reached me on top of the crane, he asked me which way the crane had been hoisting – up or down. Although I was trapped in the gearbox to a few inches below my elbow and I was in excruciating pain, I never blacked out. I told him to lower it. If I had I blacked out when the incident occurred, I would have been silently consumed by the machine. My arm was effectively sealed between the open gears, and although it may have taken some time, it was possible to wind the gears in the opposite direction and release what was left of my arm. However, in the heat of the moment the first man on the scene shouted the wrong instructions to the crane driver. He told him to "hoist up quickly". I braced myself to be released. The gearbox groaned and sprang into action again and chewed off my elbow and upper arm, tearing the skin and flesh off my upper arm and shoulder. I was yanked back towards the gears and crashed against the upright plate metal blade that was the lid of the gearbox. Had I not been wearing my safety helmet I would have been decapitated. The workman instantly realised his mistake and shouted down to the crane driver to reverse. The bloody mess of elongated and elasticated paper-thin debris of sinews and ligaments of my arm snapped out of the gears and flipped itself around my face. I slowly disentangled it. I stood and looked at what was left of my arm; it was totally destroyed and I knew it. The first thought that came into my head was that I could not play the piano anymore. This was the exercise for which I was most conscious of using my arm.

I stood on the crane, some fifty feet in the air, and squirted blood in all directions. Thank goodness I was as strong as an ox and thank goodness I was still alive. I stood and waited patiently while the medical officer was called. But he arrived at the scene and needed assistance to get back down from the gantry crane, as he was physically sick when he saw the state I was in and apparently was afraid of heights. I needed all my wits about me. Realising that I was bleeding to death like a character from a Monty Python sketch, I told one of my mates to take his dirty yellow sweater off and, while I held the cuff of one sleeve gripped against my shoulder, I told him to run around me until I screamed in agony as the makeshift tourniquet staunched the bleeding. With the bleeding stopped, my workmates laid me down on the filthy wooden floor of the bridge crane which was carpeted in a deep black layer of sand, resin and ash. At that moment, I was totally calm. I quietly said the Lord's

Prayer and waited.

The rescue operation to get me down off the crane took more than two hours and, while some had panicked, others remained calm. There were two men in particular who took control of the rescue. They were both called Gordon. One was a rigger and the other a welder. Both stood around six feet four, and I have never seen them to thank them for their efforts that day. The Fire Brigade was called to the incident, as were the police and ambulance services. A stretcher was rigged up and pulled onto the gantry. I was then strapped into it and it was lowered gingerly over the edge of the crane. There was a rope at both ends, and one in the middle, which ran right down to the ground. This was to pull me away from the metal struts of the bridge of the crane. But once over the side, the middle rope came away from the stretcher and the stretcher got caught in the struts. I could hear the two Gordons frantically discussing which one was going to get down to me in a harness to release me, but I called up and told them to lower me slowly, and I used my feet to bounce away from the bridge of the crane until I was clear of the gantry. The stretcher had tilted, so my head was above my feet, and I remember the whole rig spinning around, as the ropes entwined and I was lowered gently to the ground. I can still see the faces of the men in the casting shop transfixed, and watching the drama unfold from wherever they worked. When I reached the ground, I was met by a fireman who was very kind to me as I was taken to the waiting ambulance. Once in the ambulance, I was given oxygen and taken very rapidly, with police escort, to North Tees General Hospital. The staff set up a saline drip at the end of my bed. I asked the attractive blonde sister if they could fill it with Heineken lager – I told them I understood that "it refreshes the parts that other beers can't reach!". The pain was phenomenal but I remained calm. All the monks' advice about controlling pain came flooding back through my head. The surgeon told me that he couldn't save much of my arm. I told him to indicate on his own arm what he could save. He showed me halfway up his upper right arm. He told me he might be able to save that much. I told him to do his best. Having been contacted at work, my father rushed over to the hospital. I insisted they covered up my arm when he came in and he was asked to sign for permission to amputate, as I was still under 21. There was hardly anything left to amputate, but sadly, until only recently, my father has wrongly blamed himself for the extent of the amputation. Still tightly gripping the hand of the blonde sister, I was taken down to theatre and I was finally relieved from my ordeal. I remember the warm sensation of the general anaesthetic coursing through my veins and then, at long last, I passed out. The debris of my arm and fingers that remained on the crane was respectfully gathered up and placed in a box by the two Gordons. It was deposited in the iron furnace, and ended up in the cast iron tunnel segments that were shipped to Argentina.

CHAPTER 13

Hospital And Recovery

I regained consciousness later that afternoon and I had been transferred to the ward. I had received nine pints of blood during the operation to amputate the remains of my arm and was in substantial pain when I came to. I was strapped up, with various drips attached to my body. The acute sensation I have had in my arm from that day, is like red hot squirming maggots moving around inside my stump. Medical professionals refer to it as phantom limb pain. To the sufferer, there is nothing "phantom" about it. I use the techniques, taught to me by the monks, to shut down the pain in my stump, as well as deep concentration on something else and also resignation, recognition and acceptance of the fact that it will always be there. I remember my mother sitting at the end of my bed. I joked with her that I intended to go on a journey – but I would have to go single-handed! She burst into tears. I assured her that the main thing was that I had survived. I believe to this day that fate, or God, had equipped me to handle my predicament. I was also eternally grateful that I had actually witnessed the accident, and its consequences, and was not waking up in hospital to the terrible news. I knew how lucky I was to be alive and was counting my blessings. That night, I awoke to the prayers and mutterings of one of the priests who had been my mentor. He was giving me the last rites, just in case, and because there was a fear that I might yet die of traumatic shock. I assured him I had no plans to die. For a period of some five days, the nurses administered antibiotics intravenously every two hours, in an attempt to flush out the black grease and filth that was still in the wounds of my stump. They injected me in my thighs and backside and I was experiencing more discomfort from my aching posterior than from my amputated arm. As I was expecting to come out of the crane with the second part of the accident, I had braced myself to pull away. However, being pulled back in had torn the skin and muscle from my stump and upper shoulder and the doctors had inserted rubber drains to clean the wounds.

CHAPTER 14

Strange Coincidence

My mother came in to the hospital one day and told me of a former schoolgirl friend who had been involved in a car accident, and was now in a coma in a hospital in Hartlepool. I had not seen the girl concerned since junior school. Her name was Rachel Jones. I was preoccupied that day, as the doctors needed to remove the rubber drains from my arm. My bed was wheeled into a side ward and I was sitting up so that the surgeon could undress the stump. Doctor Ahmed informed me that he could not administer a local anaesthetic that would have any meaningful effect on the pain. I gripped the frame at the end of my bed with my good arm and told him to proceed. Instead of just pulling out the drains, he told me to brace myself and warned me "this is going to hurt".

I had to think of something to concentrate on deeply and quickly so I chose Rachel Jones's plight and prayed intensely that she would come out of the coma. My digital watch read 10.35 am. I concentrated so deeply that the surgeons performed the operation without any pain. That evening my mother came in to see me. I told her to check whether Rachel was still comatose. The following day my mother came in and told me that Rachel had come out of her coma at 10.35 the previous day. Bizarre or what!

I was in the hospital for three months and had a total of 13 operations. I had to undergo a series of skin graft operations, where skin was taken from my thighs and transplanted onto my stump. Skin graft operations are particularly painful, leaving a burning sensation at the site where the skin is taken from until it has healed. I reacted very badly to my fourth skin graft operation under general anaesthetic and the doctors were concerned that I might be going into a delayed traumatic shock. They decided to delay treatment for a few weeks while the general anaesthetic cleared my system. I was not happy, and insisted that they could perform the operations under a local anaesthetic, with me awake in the operating theatre. I discovered that the environment of the operating theatre was only a scary place because of the sterility, green outfits, and the hype that comes with watching too many hospital dramas. I would sit up and talk with the masked surgeons while they performed the skin grafts and, once back on the ward, I would immediately jump out of bed, allowing the blood to flow through the wounds on my thighs and to accelerate the healing process.

I was on the orthopaedic ward and, as such, was in the company of victims of car crashes and people who had broken their lower limbs. I was virtually the only mobile patient on the ward and thus was able to ply a roaring trade in cardboard urine bottles at 5p a go to the desperate. I fell deeply in love with at least two of the pretty student nurses and all the rest of the female staff. I made friends on the ward with an 80-year-old former coalminer from Fishburn in Co. Durham called Sid Hall and I visited him and his wife for many years later until he died. I also was able to watch the entire World Cup of 1978 while I was in hospital, although there is no truth in the rumour that I deliberately lost my arm just to see the World Cup on television. Argentina won the World Cup that year. The Pope died and John Paul I was elected Pope only to die and be succeeded by John Paul II, all while I was still in North Tees Hospital. I was overwhelmed by the kindness of my friends and relatives and the goodwill that flowed from the accident. Even the shop steward from the foundry – who had shunned me while I was working there – was obliged by the union to come and visit me with the managing director. The whole foundry had closed out of respect on the day of my accident and they had raised £376 in a whip round for me the day after. I received loads of get well cards and all the monks wrote to me individually with wise words which all helped with the healing process.

When I first stood up, having lost my arm, I was not only weak but I nearly passed out. My balance was not right and my ears popped. As soon as I was able, I insisted on doing everything myself.

I learned how to put my contact lenses in one-handed, and quickly learned how to shave myself. However when I first tried to write with my left hand, the first few letters came out as mirror writing. I believe that being naturally right handed; I was only using part of my brain. I also believe that the most dextrous task we perform is to write. I am convinced that learning to use my left hand awoke a part of my brain that had hitherto remained untapped, and that the lateral thinking involved in having to constantly dream up new ways of doing things has sharpened my sense of humour and had an enormous effect on my ability to be creative in my chosen career – advertising. I also believe that the overactive brain and some would say "imagination" that I now possess led eventually to the onset of the mental illness that has dogged the last twenty years of my life – bipolar illness or manic depression.

CHAPTER 15

Prosthetics

The stump of my arm took several months to heal and I became used to the embarrassed glances from adults and the blunt questions from children. I walked into my local pub, where the men in the back room were playing dominos. A couple of them looked up and looked away. Amputation is, after all, taboo like mental health. "See if you can win a hand for me" I joked. They all collapsed in laughter and the ice was broken. Again in another pub (where else!) before a Middlesbrough friendly football match against an Argentine team in the summer of 1978, I was greeted by a friend who knew nothing about my accident. I was wearing a black leather bomber jacket and my sleeve was tucked into the pocket. "Where's your arm?" he asked in all innocence. "It was there when I left the house" I replied as I frantically searched for it. It was a little cruel but caused much merriment.

CHAPTER 16

Tying Shoe Laces.

I was sent on a course to a hospital in Chapel Allerton in Leeds to learn how to use a prosthetic arm. I recall it was at the time when the Yorkshire Ripper was still at large and active in that area. I drove to Leeds one-handed, arrived and presented myself at the hospital. I was shocked to find that the hospital had put me up in a bed on a cardiac ward. I refused to get into my pyjamas and instead went out in Leeds, returning to the ward only to sleep and eat. In the brief time I was on the ward some seven people died and I found the whole experience both disconcerting and ironic at the same time. What a place to send someone who has just been through a near-death experience! The prosthetics trainer was called George and he was a very kind and well-meaning individual in his late sixties. What first struck me about him was that he had two arms! I was his only pupil. On the second day he told me that he would teach me how to tie my shoelaces with one hand. I was wearing trainers and both my shoes were neatly tied. I politely pointed this out to him and told him, I had invented my own technique for tying my shoelaces with one hand. He asked me to show him, so I did. Then he demonstrated another way of tying the shoes. I told him I was quite happy with my way but he was adamant that I was not doing it "the right way". When you have to achieve an objective and you learn how to think laterally, there is no right or wrong way about your method. I often tie my tie (even bow ties) one-handed as a party trick. I left Leeds with a bag full of attachments for my arm, which I used to bring out at parties. I was eventually fitted with a false arm which had a cosmetic hand to match my left one. It was very realistic indeed but extremely heavy when worn on the false arm. However, the false hand was totally useless serving only to make me blend in, until someone spotted it was not real and then became really inquisitive and embarrassed at the same time. I decided to confront the embarrassment of other people, as well as myself, by wearing a pirate's hook. I found it more functional, as I could hold things down with it and carry things on it. When I set up my advertising agency, I knew that it was the most memorable thing about any client's first meeting with me. I called the company "Hook Advertising Ltd". When the agency was doing well I even commissioned the making of a hook in solid sterling silver with three gold rings on the stem. I even had miniature 'hook and cuff' cuff links made of gold with my initials inscribed on them. The hook served to break the ice in more ways than one and became my trademark. Adults are more embarrassed than children, and I remember once being in a supermarket, when a small boy spotted my hook. He tugged at his busy mother's sleeve and whispered frantically to her. She tried to get on with her shopping but he was persistent. Eventually she stopped in her tracks and told him that it was "rude to whisper". He immediately spoke out at the top of his voice. "That man's got a hook". "Shhhhhhhh!" she replied as everyone turned and looked at them and me. I told her not to worry – it happens all the time. On another occasion my friend Kevin Connolly, who ran a catering business, asked me to do him a favour. He was owed money by a number of people for various events where he had already done the catering. I recall my friend, Duncan Walker, and myself going into a workingmen's club in Middlesbrough with Kevin. Duncan is a large and very strong man and I am quite well built. We simply stood beside Kevin while he accosted the individual who owed him money. Once again he was rebuffed; that is until Kevin made it clear he was not alone. Duncan and I slowly sipped on our beer while I tapped my hook firmly on the bar. The client immediately reached into his pocket and pulled out the money for Kevin. We collected three debts for Kevin that day, and all we had to do was drink a couple of pints and stand there. Kevin gave us a couple of quid too.

CHAPTER 17

First Experience Of Litigation

The Transport and General Workers Union was the main union in the iron foundry, but the shop steward of the foundry was determined not to let me become a member. He never remembered to bring any forms for me to fill in and constantly complained that I was a student keeping another union member out of a job. After several weeks of his avoiding the issue (and me), I took matters into my own hands and joined the T&G at its office in Stockton-on-Tees. Thus, when my accident took place, the sour-faced and brusque shop steward found himself having to represent me, whether he liked it or not. My industrial accident was my first experience of the civil courts, but my compensation was sorted out by the union, its lawyers and the company in a way that suited them, perhaps more than it suited me. By that I mean that had I known then what I know these days, about civil litigation, I would not have settled for the £23,000 that was eventually offered. I was young and quite frankly naïve, and was determined to recover as soon as possible rather than dwell on the potentially protracted litigation process. It is a small price indeed for the virtual total loss of a main arm. I became a number on an insurance file without realising it, and knew little or nothing about the processes of loss-adjusters. I innocently went along with the indignity of men in suits measuring my stump with tape measures. I was awarded £500 in compensation for not being able to play the piano any more. The Health and Safety Executive prosecuted the owners of the iron foundry. Following my accident, new safety procedures were brought in for the isolation of machinery with mesh grids and guards installed to prevent fingers even being able to reach into machines. I was not required to be at the hearing where the foundry was prosecuted but attended anyway. I did not need to attend as they were pleading guilty to the charges and had brought in a barrister to plead mitigation. I sat at the back of the court and listened. The female barrister described me as a young man of ethnic origin, who had perhaps not understood the English instructions too well. The foundry was praised for its policy of employing Asian workers. The barrister pointed me out to the Court and said I was a student who would certainly use his brains more than his hands. As I had no right of reply, I was forced to ask the Health and Safety people to request that I could meet the magistrates for a short word in chambers. I very quickly established my articulacy and pointed out that it would be nice to still have the choice to use my hands as well as my brains. Nevertheless, the foundry was fined a measly £250. However, following my accident, the foundry was permitted to finish off its contract and was then shut permanently. It was demolished a couple of years later and is now a housing development.

CHAPTER 18

Diamonds Are For Never

I went to an investment adviser with my compensation. We chewed over various possibilities. The one that sticks in my mind was to invest in a diamond in Amsterdam. Apparently you could buy a diamond. The diamond would be safely kept for you in Amsterdam and you could visit it whenever you wanted. Apparently you got a certificate of ownership. I pointed out that I could not tell the difference between one diamond and another and that the people who sold the diamond could sell the same diamond many times over and probably get away with it. There also seemed to be something vaguely ridiculous about travelling to Amsterdam to visit my diamond. Instead, I bought a house in my parents' village of Norton-on-Tees and rented it out. I did not want the hassle of being a landlord, so I put it in the hands of estate agents and rented it out to business people. Every Christmas, I would turn up at the house and present my tenants with a hamper. It was good PR. I never had any trouble with them.

CHAPTER 19

The Grate Cheese Robbery

My recovery meant that I missed the opportunity to return to university the following year. I got a job in a local cheese factory. It was really more of a warehouse, distributing the entire variety of cheeses you see in supermarkets. A fleet of lorries criss-crossed the country making deliveries and sales, while a group of young lads made up the various orders for the lorry drivers, laying out the cheeses on wooden pallets. There was also a Cryovac area where old returns were pared down and repacked in sealed polythene bags or converted into grated cheese packs for use by bakeries and caterers. My job was to check the stock on the vans and make sure the lorry drivers were only loading what was in their orders. Cheese is a very expensive commodity and was worth a fortune on the black market. The whole cheeses were extremely heavy, like different sized drums and, depending on the variety, came down in size to a baby cheese that you could hold with one hand. One of the young factory lads was hit on the head by a baby Wensleydale that fell off a pallet from one of the high storage shelves in the factory. I took him to hospital as he was concussed. He was extremely embarrassed about how he had been injured when he had to admit to the doctors that he had been felled by a cheese. My job was not particularly taxing and I mentioned this to the Managing Director. Big mistake! He asked me to conduct an undercover investigation into the stock system from the point where the cheeses got onto the vans and then report back on his suspicions that some of the drivers were fiddling the company out of serious amounts of money. His suspicions were indeed, well founded. My clandestine research showed me that virtually the entire team of lorry drivers was on the fiddle, making a small fortune out of this "perishable" product. However, I was reluctant to report them by name, as the corruption was far reaching and it would have meant that I could not face them day after day and practically continue in the job. Also, if the drivers were sacked, it would take months to replace them and rebuild the relationships they had with their customers as well as the knowledge required to do the job. Therefore, I introduced an ostensibly random method of checking the stock onto the vans and into the content of the vans themselves. It was impossible to check all the stock but the drivers simply did not know what they could get away with fiddling, so they stopped rather than take the chance of being caught. The Managing Director was delighted with the diplomatic way it was all handled. He did not press me for any names and I did not volunteer any.

Chapter 20

Back To University

I returned to the University of Liverpool at the end of my two-year sabbatical. I was a mature student. My experiences over the last two years had made me so. I changed course to do a combined degree in French and Communications studies, as I was hoping to eventually work in the media, either as a journalist or in the field of advertising. Then I met my wife-to-be, Helen. I had spotted her in the National Westminster bank standing in a queue. She was a beautiful brunette. Then I ran into her again. I went to the well attended first meeting of the French Society in one of the lecture theatres and was sitting at the back waiting for the meeting to come to order, when who should walk in but the same NatWest pretty brunette. We exchanged a few words. She later told me she had thought me extremely cocky for a first year student. Then she walked to the front of the lecture theatre and called the meeting to attention. It turned out she was the elected president of the French Society that year. Within a few days, we were in love and had some wonderful years courting. When we had finished our university courses, we eventually moved to London, married and have three wonderful children; identical twin daughters, Caitlin and Rebecca, and a son, Leo. Unfortunately the mental illness that has dogged my life for the last twenty years utterly devastated our relationship and means we are now divorced. I live back in the North of England, while Helen and the kids live in Surrey. I do not lay any blame whatsoever at her door for the breakdown in our marriage or relationship. I recognise that I became unbearable during the latter years of our marriage, and that she found herself looking after four children rather than just three. She will always be a major part of my life and, as the mother of my children, will always hold a special place in my heart. She is a very private person and I hope this book causes her no further embarrassment.

CHAPTER 21

An Advertising Career

My career in advertising started at a small agency called GDA, who were specialists in advertising commercial property. I offered my services to them for the first six weeks unpaid, with a further incentive of a weekly benefit of £45, which was paid to them for taking on a registered disabled person. I had been directed to them by Saatchi and Saatchi Advertising. They had interviewed me and had found me too mature for the junior account executives roles that were usually filled by young graduates. I was quickly promoted and rewarded and, within eleven months, I became new business director of the agency; with a brief to expand their portfolio of clients outside the property market. I won some work with Vichy, the cosmetics company, and Marks and Spencer and ICL, the computer giant. I was developing a reputation for my creative approaches and pitches to clients. Then I approached a record company called Starblend which had a portfolio of compilation albums. As GDA were not geared to handle television media buying, we brought in a Saatchi and Saatchi satellite media company to help us pitch for the account. Thus a friendship was forged between me and the principals of that company. In the dog-eat-dog world of advertising, I was headhunted by the Saatchi Company and became their in-house new business and creative consultant. I was paid a fee and had access to all the resources of the Saatchi Empire and they paid all my overheads. I set up Hook Advertising Limited; named after the steel hook that I wore on my false right arm. It was one feature that a client never forgets. I would pitch for, and creatively make approaches to, all types of clients working with the new business department of Saatchi, usually going for the most reluctant clients. If a client said no to Saatchi, sometimes because of their political persuasion, I would approach them and try to coax them through the door. On more than one occasion, I commissioned a 48 sheet (20 x 10 feet) poster on the route a potential client took to work and addressed him by name directly through the poster. Imagine the surprise – and impact – of a billboard, or say a personalised radio commercial, congratulating you by name on your birthday as you were driving to work. It was my job to get a foot in the door, and I was given creative carte blanche as to how to approach it.

CHAPTER 22

We Believe In Advertising

I decided to run corporate advertising for Hook Advertising in the marketing journals and other periodicals. One moody black and white advertisement featured a man, of about thirty years of age, in a black suit and tie, wearing a pair of glasses and carrying a copy of *The Times* under his arm. He had a badge on his lapel that read "CLIENT" and bore a striking resemblance to Clark Kent. Everything about him was upright, confident and impeccable, and he appeared to be posing as if admiring himself in a mirror. But his flies were undone and his shirt tail was hanging out. Our headline read "SOME AGENCIES WOULDN'T TELL HIM". We were attacking the concept of the subservient agency, who just agreed with their clients and did not have the guts, or the know-how, to work on an equal footing with their clients and give them a truly professional opinion, whether they liked it or not. I know that some agencies at the time were deeply critical of the advertisement, and phoned us up to tell us so. More importantly, we won clients directly from the advertising and became high-profile and included on new clients' pitch lists overnight. Our slogan on all our advertising ran "HOOK ADVERTISING – WE BELIEVE IN ADVERTISING".

Man with flies undone – Photo Steve Gale

CHAPTER 23

Flash Cars

When I lost my arm, many people told my parents, with great authority, that I would not be able to drive again. As soon as I left hospital, I bought a blue automatic Mini Cooper and escaped in it to see my various friends around the country to the concern of my parents' neighbours. To give them their due, my parents just decided to let me get on with living my life. While on my year off recuperating after the accident, I worked with a friend on building a kit car. It was called a Merlin TF and closely resembled a Morgan. My friend, Don Sayer, was a mechanic by trade, and he was delighted to be given the opportunity to build a car and be paid for it as well. Along with another of my best friends, Duncan Walker, who had lived in the house next to my parents' house since I was born, Don and I travelled from the North-east to Southend-on-Sea in a huge Luton van that we had hired to pick up the car's body shell, that was made of fibreglass and the chassis, that was made of steel. Having examined and checked the shell of the car, it was time to pay. The cost of the shell and chassis alone was some £3000. To the astonishment of all present, I unscrewed my false arm to reveal a cavity between my elbow and the end of my stump. Inside the cavity was the £3000 in rolled-up cash. The cream Merlin was indeed a flash car and I cut quite a dash in it when I returned to Liverpool to do my degree, but it paled into insignificance when compared with the cars I would drive later in my advertising career. As soon as Hook started to make a healthy profit, I bought a car that went with the image of a successful advertising agency. It was a white Porsche 924 and I went straight back up to the North-east of England to park it outside my parents' end of terrace house to the complete bewilderment of the doubting neighbours and much to the delight of my mates. I then moved on to a Mediterranean Blue Lotus Excel SA with a plush cream leather interior. That car was a truly beautiful machine: made as it was out of fibreglass, it was light and extremely manoeuvrable and responsive, especially on the motorways. I had been to the "Motor Show" at Earls Court the previous year and had seen and bought the Lotus right off their exhibition stand. To my misfortune, it was delivered the day after I broke my leg so I had to wait a while to drive it.

As the business was doing so well, and we had just bagged our biggest account (the Rabbit/BYPS account I shall refer to later) in August 1989, I decided to upgrade my car yet again. I bought a brand new red convertible Maserati Spyder Biturbo for £40,000 from a dealer in Berkeley Square in London W1. It was a beautiful car to behold and it went like a rocket. However, it broke down four times during the first three weeks of my ownership. On each occasion I was on the motorway on my way to a meeting and I was obliged to return in the cab of a recovery vehicle. Initially I was patient and was prepared to put it down to teething problems, but the more it happened, the less confident I felt that I could trust the car to get me from A to B. On the last occasion it broke down, the dealer's mechanics installed a flick switch on two loose wires in the boot of the car. They said that they had rigged up a system to bypass the electric ignition system in the event of breakdown and that all I had to do if the car failed was to pull over and give it five minutes before flicking the switch. I pointed out to them that this car had cost me £40,000 and that even the cheapest car on the road did not have such a switch in its boot. I simply could not trust the car and I was not impressed by their Heath Robinson method of fixing the problem, so I asked them politely for my money back. They refused, saying that they had never given anyone their money back in their history and they were adamant that they were not about to start now. They said that they would continue to repair the car as it was under warranty. They said that were I to take legal action then the matter would take years to come to court. I decided to make a few phone calls. Three days later a giant mobile billboard arrived outside their showroom in Mayfair. On the poster, printed on both sides, it read "BETTER THAN TALKING TO ESTHER?" (a reference to the BBC's successful consumer watchdog programme "That's Life" that was hosted by Esther Rantzen). The copy went on to say. "We bought a brand new Maserati Spyder Biturbo from James Young Specialist Cars. It broke down on 2nd August, then it broke down on 4th August, then it broke down on 15th August, then it broke down on 20th August. We want our money back. We think we'll buy a Ford." The effect was instantaneous. The tabloid press and television stations descended on us in a media maelstrom. The nature of the protest was discussed on national and local television and radio, and experts were wheeled in to comment from the Consumers' Association. Then came the police. Apparently they had been called by the shocked car-dealers to come and arrest me for "libel". I sat them down and made them a cup of tea and told them the facts and they realised they could not intervene in a civil dispute in any event. They were concerned, however, that the mobile billboard was holding up the traffic in Mayfair, as crowds stopped to read it. They asked for permission to escort the vehicle around the area with a police bike with flashing lights. I was delighted and gave them my blessing as that drew even more attention to the convoy. As for the car dealer, despite not having many customers during the two days of the poster protest, they decided to sit tight and weather the storm. The Managing Director emphasised, yet again, that he would not budge and certainly would not give us our money back. He pointed out what I already knew – that today's news is tomorrow's fish and chip paper – so I telephoned the Marketing Director of Maserati in Italy, who knew all about the dispute, to advise him of my next move. I told him truthfully that we had been contacted by 32 other disgruntled Maserati car owners, who all had problems with their cars breaking down. I was planning a Maserati owners' protest rally in Berkeley Square next to the dealer. I pointed out that the car belonged to me, so I could do with it what I pleased. When it was time to freshen the message, I would not hesitate. I told him that the following day, I intended to park my Maserati in my parking bay at Soho Square. We intended to take the top off this beautiful piece of junk, and fill the sumptuous cream leather upholstery and the whole car using an earth remover and a lorry full of soil. We would then plant a pine tree in the car and place on it a huge banner that read, "MASERATI – Probably the most expensive plant pots in the world". We would turn the whole thing into a huge media event. Maserati gave us our money back.

CHAPTER 24

The Devil's In The Detail

One time, I was driving back from the North-west of England to London, in the early hours of the morning in a Porsche. We had been shooting some footage of the first laser technology to be used in a night-club, for our client First Leisure Corporation, for whom we did a lot of work, especially in opening discotheques. I had been invited to go to the FA Cup Final that day and there was no traffic on the road. Suddenly, I noticed a blue flashing light in my rear-view mirror. It was a white Jaguar motorway patrol car. I pulled over, and I sat in the car as I was approached by a female officer. She was alone. She told me that I had been speeding and, having taken my details, she warned me to slow down, which I did. A couple of months later, I received a summons to go to a magistrates court in the Midlands. Having thoroughly read through the court documents, I decided to go and defend myself. My lawyer at the time told me I was wasting my time, and that the penalty might be even higher for wasting the court's time. Nevertheless, I travelled through to the court and arrived early in the morning. I had hired a mobile phone from one of my clients "Fonehire", so that I could stay in touch with the office. Those were the days when portable phones were the size of house bricks. Outside the court, intermediaries ran between lawyers and potential clients because, at the time, solicitors were not allowed to solicit for business directly. I rejected their approaches and elected to defend myself. Once in the court, I had the Clerk of the Court read out the charge. Then I had him read it out again, and yet again to be sure that that was what they were charging me with. I pleaded not guilty, and was asked what my defence was. I replied with "I was never on the northbound carriageway on the day in question". I was asked to repeat my answer several times. Eventually, the Clerk of the Court muttered under his breath, "He must have been on the southbound carriageway". I replied: "That's not what I'm accused of". The barrister for the police requested that the charge be changed, but I vehemently objected and the magistrates agreed that they could only hear the charge that was in the writ of summons. Then the Clerk of the Court advised me that I should ask the magistrates to dismiss the charge. The magistrates agreed, and I asked that the police pay my costs for travelling to the Court, and for hiring the mobile phone. My opponents received a severe ticking off from the Chief Magistrate for wasting the Court's time and a couple of months later, I received a cheque for some £275 for my costs.

CHAPTER 25

Premises Not Promises

In the mid-to-late eighties, renting office space cost a small fortune. I found some ground floor offices for Hook in Soho Square, London W1. The only trouble was that the landlords (who shall remain nameless, except for the fact that they were the biggest in the UK at the time) wanted us to pay them a £75,000 premium over and above the rent. It was a landlords' market and they could gratuitously, just about, name their price. We could afford the rent, but not the premium. What struck me about the offices as soon as I saw them were the huge hexagonal pillars, the tops of which could only be seen above your head, which were divided off and virtually concealed by the stained brown office partitioning. Knock these partitions down and there would be plenty of open plan space and light for executives and designers. The offices were dilapidated and had been the home for a textile company for more than thirty years. A once successful business, employing some fifty people, was now reduced to a little old man and his two elderly female assistants rattling around in what had evolved into a honeycomb of dark little cell-like offices. The other side of the building was occupied by a courier company and there were the skeletons of stripped motorbikes and pushbikes in every corridor, with oil and black grease wiped on every wall along with occasional mounds of rubbish. The plaster was coming down from the ceilings, wires hung exposed from the ceilings and walls and the overall effect was one of dinginess and darkness. I said that I was interested in the premises for my advertising agency and had reluctantly accepted the terms in principle. A week into the prospective deal, I phoned the estate agent and told him that I was getting cold feet because of the filthy state of the premises, so we arranged a meeting with the landlord and his agent at the offices at Soho Square to discuss my concerns. The estate agent said he alone would attend but I insisted that the landlord was present. We met in the morning and shook hands. We were all dressed in smart city suits and I remember, I was wearing a silk Dennis the Menace tie. Then we entered the building. As we walked into the entrance, I pointed out the terrible state of the foyer. Piles of rubble and rubbish lay scattered down the main corridor leading to the offices. The landlord and his agent were munching croissants and drinking coffee as we entered the corridor. Suddenly, from the darkest reaches of the corridor, there came a loud moaning sound. Then the dust and rubbish bags in one corner seemed to move and the moaning turned into a loud series of curses interspersed with coughing. From within the rubble and plaster and waste appeared the filthy figure of a tramp in a long dirty raincoat, clutching a bundle of carrier bags which sounded as if they were full of bottles. He seemed not to see us at first and proceeded to urinate against the wall. Then he spotted us and roared at us. We had clearly woken him up and he was not pleased. My companions dropped their food, turned tail and fled up the corridor in the opposite direction, with me not far behind them. Once in the foyer, one of the old ladies from the textile company came rushing out and cried "He's been here all morning, are you from the landlords?" The landlord said he would call the police. I told him not to waste police time. I explained that my time as a bouncer in the nightclub had made me unperturbed by the situation. I went back down the corridor and gave the tramp a couple of quid to move on and buy a cup of tea and some food. He stank of alcohol and urine. He took the money and slowly dragged himself and his carrier bags away. When I returned, the landlord and the estate agent were full of praise and apologies. However, I was not satisfied with an apology. I berated the slick landlord's representative and told him, in no uncertain terms that I was no longer prepared to go ahead with the deal. I calmly pointed out that unless they refurbished the offices, they would have little chance renting them out to anyone, let alone an advertising agency that relied upon the right image to attract the right clients. Indeed, I told them that the sort of client I might expect in the future would be the down-and-out who had made himself so comfortable in their squalor. The landlord was beginning to think on his feet and volunteered a reduction in the premium to £50,000. I refused and he carried on negotiating. Eventually we agreed to a rent only deal with no premium at all and a refurbishment of the premises to boot. I accepted, on condition that the revised terms were on my desk within the hour. I returned to the agency and waited. Forty minutes later there was a fax on my desk from the estate agent, confirming the new deal. Approximately one hour later the tramp came into our offices in Goodge Street. We let him clean himself up in the gents and then I paid him his £200 fee. He was an actor that we had hired from a casting agency. We had selected him because he looked like a thug who was down on his luck, somebody you would not want to meet down a dark alley. The rest was make-up, oversized clothes and a disgusting raincoat and we had placed a ripe stinking Camembert cheese in his pockets, to make him smell. Over a cup of well-earned coffee and a sandwich, he told us that he had experienced great difficulty dragging himself around in the oversized lace-less shoes we had got for him. His most difficult moments were when he was waiting at the little hut in Soho Square for the office doors to open so he could get in. Apparently he had been harangued for wasting his life by some "well-meaning" evangelical Christians, while at the same time he was touched by the generosity of the other vagrants who wanted to share their wine bottles and lager cans with him. I hired an actor to perform this role because I simply couldn't have trusted a real tramp with the stage directions. He told me that it was the hardest and most enjoyable role he had ever played. His only regret was that nobody witnessed the performance.

CHAPTER 26

Break A Leg

As a consultant to the Saatchi & Saatchi Empire, I had the pleasure of being invited to their terrific company parties. However, every year the parties would become more outrageous and, indeed, potentially dangerous. In 1987 they outdid themselves and decided to hold the party at an ice rink. The cocktail of excellent bucks fizz and food and the spectacle of a live game of ice hockey during the evening, certainly attracted me. I remember my wife, Helen, warning me before I set out that night, not to go on the ice. The party was just open to Saatchi employees and there were no wives or girlfriends present. Nevertheless I sat at a table next to the ice and drank in the chilly atmosphere and the free champagne. As the alcohol coursed through my system, I watched with envy as the skaters glided past my table. Then, the temptation became too great. Two very pretty blonde Saatchi employees skated up to where I was sitting and invited me onto the ice. My protestation was unconvincing and did not last very long. I forgot the excellent advice of my wife. The alcohol, and the glamorous girls and my male ego had convinced me. I was up for it. A couple of minutes later, I had laced up a pair of skates and I gingerly tottered over to the ice to join the girls. One held out her hand. Literally, as I stepped onto the ice, my right skate twisted to the left, while my torso twisted to the right. Although I am now left-handed, I am still right-sided in my head. My natural reaction was to fall to my right hand side. I fell onto the ice and my right leg snapped like a twig, between the knee and the ankle, and collapsed. I knew immediately that my leg was broken, and persuaded my concerned companions to leave me where I was. A fellow director, skated over and confirmed the worst. He said he had seen it before on a rugby field. An ambulance was called, and I was carefully stretchered off the ice and was taken to a hospital in Paddington. The doctors set the bones that night despite my having consumed so much alcohol. When I awoke the following morning, I was in a room with three other orthopaedic male patients and I was in plaster from my ankle up to the top of my thigh. My false arm was on a chair next to my bed, and the net effect was that half of my body didn't work! I was not fazed by my predicament. I called one of my clients "Fonehire" who, not surprisingly, hired out mobile phones, albeit big mobile phones, and a phone was immediately delivered to my bedside. If I couldn't walk, I would run my business from my bed. I had many a business meeting in a room on the ward that wasn't being used, and my staff had plenty of initiative and could be trusted to carry on without me. Saatchis got a bashing from some uninvited journalists for the excesses of the Saatchi party and my accident was reported by some of the national broadsheets. When I asked Saatchi whether they were insured for my injury, they were keen to help out in every way. When I recovered, they even laid on a chauffeur-driven limousine to take me wherever I wanted.

CHAPTER 27

Before Viagra

While in hospital, I quickly learned to master a wheelchair one – handed and I used to wheel myself from bed to bed, and chat with the other patients. There was one particular patient called Errol who, like me, had been involved in an industrial accident. He had been catapulted out of a crane that collapsed on a building site. He had injured his back and the fall had concertinaed various vertebrae. He was a tall, black, muscular man in his early twenties. I was able to offer him useful advice about his own accident, and help him to understand the legal side of what would follow his discharge. We had become good friends. Errol was permanently strapped to a special orthopaedic bed that looked like two old penny-farthing bicycles stuck together, with a mattress slung between them. He lived on the bed. The bed revolved and had a series of weights attached to it that stretched his spine. Errol was either on his back, or his front and horizontal, or vertical as they treated him and exercised him during each day. His parents and family used to come from Brixton each day to see him. Errol was a model patient, and was polite to everyone who looked after him. But to add to the discomfort of his injuries, Errol could not move away from his corner. Anyone who has been incapacitated for a while and is bedridden will identify with Errol. You become a target for all the do-gooders, hospital visitors, and religious extremists, who invite themselves to your bedside to sit and talk to you. Errol was such a target. One day, however, I wheeled myself over to Errol's bedside for a chat. He told me to f*** off. Then he said it to one of the nurses, and finally he lost his temper with the consultant. I made a few enquiries and discovered that he was upset that he was to be transferred to the spinal injuries hospital at Stoke Mandeville. He was furious that his family would not be able to visit him daily as he had been used to. He was in a terrible mood and kept shouting at everyone who approached him "It's ok for you, nothing on my f***ing body works". At exactly 5.30 pm that afternoon, the nurses came in and tilted Errol's bed so that he was vertical. "Leave me alone," he protested "This isn't the f***ing right time". The nurses told Errol that he had a visitor. Errol politely protested that he just wanted to be left alone. But it was too late. In walked a plump Carmelite nun in full habit. She looked around the room, and then walked straight to Errol's bed. She parked herself beside him and started to mutter prayers for him. Then, lifting her head, she began to harangue him at the top of her voice in a thick Irish brogue. Errol politely protested that he just wanted to be left alone. But the nun was adamant. Apparently Errol was the father of her unborn child and she wanted him to take responsibility for its upbringing. The sound of the commotion attracted the attention of both staff, and visitors and a small crowd gathered around Errol's bed. Suddenly, the nun pulled a cushion from under her robes and, with the expertise of the Equity card holding actress and stripper she was, she deftly removed the rest of her garb. Blonde and beautiful, she stood stark naked except for her red fishnet stockings, suspenders and stilettos, right in front of the perplexed Errol. Errol was clad in nothing but a plain white sheet which, to his horror, embarrassment, and eventual glee, started to rise. He simply couldn't help himself. He had an enormous erection and a broad toothy grin all over his face. He called me a b***tard and I laughed back at him from my wheelchair. I told him that it was good to see that at least part of his body was fully functional. Amanda, the stripping nun covered Errol in lipstick kisses and, having received her cash fee from me, she left the hospital. You couldn't wipe the smile off Errol's face for the last days of his stay. His whole mood had lightened. He was convinced he would recover. He was transferred to Stoke Mandeville for the rest of his recovery and I met him several months later when he came to visit me. His attitude was positive and he was fully fit again.

CHAPTER 28

One Left Wellie

It took many months in plaster for my bones to heal and, after a period of time in the wheelchair, I had to somehow get around on crutches. I locked my false arm into a vertical position and attached a universal heavy-duty tool-holding device from the crutch grip to the arm. The pain of supporting my weight through my stump and right shoulder was excruciating at first, but eventually I got used to it. While still in hospital, Hook was approached by a property developer to pitch for the marketing of a multi-million pound industrial site outside Sunbury, just off the M3. For all the posturing and pride of the developer and his agent, the reality was that his industrial and commercial office development, was no more exciting than anyone else's. We decided to tell him so. To somehow capture the attention and imagination of our target audience of estate agents, we needed to intrigue and to amuse. We pitched an idea for a campaign that was a piece of lateral thinking. I was amused by the fact that I now only needed one slipper, and inspired by my broken right leg, I came up with the "One left wellie" campaign. I don't know what today's commercial property market is like, but in the late eighties the price of success for an estate agent could be very high indeed. Huge incentives like sports cars and very expensive holidays and gifts, were being offered to successful estate agents almost on a weekly basis. We did not have that size of a marketing budget and we won the project from the four agencies that pitched, because our proposal was comparatively inexpensive. I decided to pitch the cost of our fee very high, with all the actual costs charged at cost. But we still came in less than our agency competitors. The developer and his agent were brave enough to run with our crazy logic. We came up with a plan to intrigue the estate agents and instantly capture awareness and response. We insisted our clients did some homework, and we narrowed the field of prospective interested agents to 50 key named individuals from fifty top firms. On the Friday, we despatched a team of glamorous promotion girls all around London. The girls went to the offices of the different agents and, while posing briefly for a photograph with the named estate agent, handed him one left "Hunter" Wellington boot. The girls were specifically not briefed as to the reason for their strange mission, so the agents who received the boots were completely baffled. Word went round the property market that day that something was "afoot" but nobody knew what. Agents who did not receive boots were equally confused as to why they had not. The next day the "Estates Gazette", the bible of the property market, was published and delivered to their homes. We had named all the individuals who had received a Wellington boot alongside a large photograph of one green "Hunter" left wellie, with a sticker on it that read "SIBC" (Sunbury International Business Centre) in a double-page spread advertisement. "WHAT POSSIBLE USE IS ONE LEFT WELLIE?" read the headline on the advertisement. The copy went on to point out, that it was of no use at all without the right one (and in the right size) but that the only way to pick up the right one was phone up and arrange to visit the development which was "a bit muddy, so you'll need a pair of wellies". The top agents all wore the "Hunter" brand and they were flattered indeed to be named, and numbered, among the top fifty. Also, and more importantly, they would kill for a free pair of "Hunter" wellies and, tongue in cheek or not, it made an amusing change to the usual incentive. The campaign was a huge success. Forty-eight out of the fifty named agents picked up their right wellies at the development site. We had, of course, produced a glossy brochure full of artists' impressions and we had picked out the site itself on the motorway with a forest of international flags around its perimeter. Hook's rifle-shot campaign (96% response, 100% awareness – our client steadfastly refused to give the other two right boots to the agents who rang up but would not go to the site) cost significantly less than the shotgun approach that our competitors would have done. We won four top advertising and marketing awards later that year for the campaign.

HOW TO GET 96% RESPONSE AND WIN 4 GOLD I.S.P. AWARDS

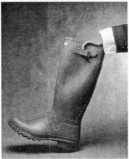

WITH ONE WELLIE AND A LOT OF SAVVY

HOOK
ADVERTISING

12/14 WHITFIELD STREET LONDON W1P 5RA
TELEPHONE 01 436 5556

CREATIVE ADVERTISING... THAT WORKS

One left wellie – Photo Steve Gale

I remember the award ceremony vividly because I had to hobble up to the stage on my false arm/crutch to pick up the awards. The atmosphere and the champagne proved to be great painkillers. More importantly, the "Sunbury International Business Centre" was high profile, and pre-let within weeks of the campaign through one of the agents we had targeted.

CHAPTER 29

Non-PC plcs

The advertising world is a fun place, whatever type of clients the agency may have. But for me, a red-blooded male, the best accounts we had were, what I called, the 'glamour' accounts. We had work with a swimwear and lingerie client, as well as a swimming pool manufacturer. One of the perks of the job of Chairman and Creative Director of the agency, was overseeing photographic shoots and selecting gorgeous women from the numerous talent agencies we employed. However, the most glamorous day I ever had in the business, was when a PLC company property client, whose hobbies included collecting Ferraris and Pirelli calendars decided to do a calendar for his PLC property company. We mocked up a calendar that featured naked women posing in the environs of twelve of the property company's developments. Then, we organised a casting session at one of our photographer's studios. We were expecting the client to turn up by himself but, when he arrived, he had brought three of his friends with him. These included his favourite estate agent, his accountant, and his lawyer. During a period of six hours, 40 glamour girls from different modelling agencies arrived and stripped down to the bare essentials for our photographer, Steve. The client's friends pretended to be from my advertising agency and gave themselves titles, like art director and copywriter, to the girls. Then, all of a sudden, one of the girls came round the screen we had erected to give the girls some privacy. She approached the client and his friends and introduced herself. They presented her with their phoney titles and she turned to one of them and said "No, you're not an art director; you're my lawyer!" The lawyer turned bright red, but, having been rumbled, elected to have his photograph taken with his model client draped round him in a James Bond pose. In the event, the property client never made the calendar but we were paid handsomely for a day which we would have gladly participated in for free.

One of our other clients was First Leisure Corporation plc who owned nightclubs and discotheques around the country. They used to hold a glamour competition for would-be models all round the country, called Miss "In String". For this competition, the contestants would compete for the title wearing nothing but sexy costumes made of string-vest like material. Their costumes left little, or nothing, to the imagination. One day, I was invited to the Empire at Leicester Square to be a judge in the Grand Final of the event. My other fellow judges included a Page Three girl and Eddie Kidd, the dare devil stunt rider. The compere introduced us to the packed nightclub. "We have Samantha from Page Three looking for new talent for Page Three (applause), Eddie Kidd looking for a co-star for his movie (applause), and Chris Joseph, Chairman of Hook Advertising…looking for a pair of scissors! (Rapturous applause and loud cheering)". There was nothing politically correct about either of my clients, or indeed any of the clients I ever worked for. They hired us because we could sell them better than their competition, and they fired us if we ever let them down. Anyone ever considering entering the world of advertising, should be aware that it is the most competitive environment, where you are only as good as your next bright idea and there is little place for the moral high ground.

CHAPTER 30

Hook Lands Big Fish With Rabbit

In 1989, the British government handed out four licenses to various consortia to produce a mass-market mobile telephone system called "telepoint". The technology to be used was CT2, or the second generation of cordless telephones using the DECT digital cordless system. People already had cordless analogue telephones in their homes, but the DECT phones would work anywhere within three hundred metres of a base station or transmitter/receiver. The idea was for all four consortia to compete for customers on their own networks, and eventually set up roaming deals so that customers using CT2 could use their phones whenever in range of any network provider. Through his contacts, Hook's new business director, Hugo Tewson, got us on to the pitch list for the Mercury Communications consortium, but we stood little or no chance of winning the business, as Mercury were keen to appoint their current agency, who were handling all the Mercury branded business as the government sought to break up the British Telecom monopoly. We did a presentation at Mercury's offices, but it was obvious from their reaction that we were just there to make up the numbers. We were quickly informed that we had not been successful and the ever-resourceful Hugo quickly made the calls to get us onto the pitch list for the only consortium that had not yet chosen an agency: the consortium of Barclays Bank, Philips Electronics, and Shell Ventures eventually known as "BYPS". They were allowing five agencies (including the advertising agencies from the parent companies) to pitch for the business and allowed us to become the sixth as we had pitched for the Mercury Consortium. We had less than a week to get ready. I had been invited to stay at a De Vere Hotel in Coventry, where Hook was helping Schwarzkopf to launch a new range of hair products. My creative director, Rob, and I sat in the empty bar drinking copious amounts of coffee. We both agreed that the techno-sounding names adopted by the other consortia for their systems would be very confusing, and felt that a customer could quite easily go out and subscribe to the wrong service. We also felt that this was the opportunity to stand out from the crowd. As we bounced ideas off each other, I suggested that we needed something warm and friendly to attract what would eventually be a mass-market product. I suggested a Rabbit or even a Parrot. I wrote the word "Rabbit" on my pad with a capital "R". I had studied Russian, while at school, and was used to seeing a mirrored "R" in my mind's eye. Then I inverted the pad, and put a dot in the hole in the "R". It was a graphic representation of a Rabbit's head with its ears sticking out. I drew a rectangle around the inverted "R", and recognised immediately that we had a logo. I went back to Soho Square and instructed the graphic designers to draw up a campaign around the "Rabbit" name and logo.

Rabbit logo – Photo Chris Joseph

A couple of days later, we made our pitch at the Savoy Hotel in the Strand to the various representatives of the BYPS consortium. They had decided not to show any emotion in the pitch, but we learned afterwards that they were absolutely delighted with our ideas and had struggled not to jump out of their seats and shout "Eureka"!

Chapter 31

Big Is Beautiful

After the pitch, the Barclays Philips Shell Consortium Company (BYPS) was making all the right noises. I knew that their daily regular contacts by phone meant that we were on the verge of winning what would be significantly the largest single piece of business in Hook Advertising's brief history. BYPS Executive Directors came from the parent companies with the operating directors selected from a team of executives, primarily from Philips, who were supposed to bring their technological wizardry to the party. Barclays and Shell were supposed to provide sites for the telepoint transmitters or base-stations, but in the event, Shell later found out it could not site the transmitters on its forecourts because they were a fire hazard; what you might call a slight oversight! However, although they were clearly delighted by our 'Rabbit' pitch, the executives from Shell decided that to avoid showing they were too keen, and to attempt to counterbalance our strong negotiating position, they would make an inspection of our premises and our books. They were to send in their financial director – a David Newman – and he would make the inspection. I thought this was unfair as our "Rabbit" idea was clearly streets ahead of the other agencies with whom we were competing. Fortunately for us, the corporate giants that constituted BYPS were used to setting up appointments, and they gave us forty-eight hours to prepare. I knew that as Hook, at that time, was only a small company employing perhaps ten people and a few freelancers, BYPS would seek to intimidate us, saying they needed a larger agency with a longer track record, a bigger portfolio and accounts that showed more substantial turnover and longevity – ironically precisely what the BYPS consortium did not have when we sought to credit insure them when they nearly went belly up a couple of years later. Nevertheless, we did have 48 hours before the inspection. We started our preparations to make a large and convincing agency illusion for the visiting Mr Newman. We arranged to pick him up at the offices of Shell in a chauffeur–driven limousine. He arrived at Soho Square and was greeted at the door by the commissionaire in full uniform, who saluted him and lead him through the long reception up to the reception desk. The normally bare walls of the corridor were covered in examples of our work and paintings. Large potted plants were dotted at intervals. We had brought in sumptuous leather Chesterfield couches and, to the obvious delight and distraction of Mr Newman, leggy models clutching portfolios in miniskirts chattered nervously on the seats. The very attractive receptionist offered Mr Newman a glass of wine while he was waiting, and he was pleased to accept. We kept him waiting for a couple of minutes and then phoned my secretary to announce his arrival. I came out and greeted him. Although we had never met before, I recognised and mentioned his Geordie accent which still could just be detected through his London accent. The agency was absolutely buzzing. People were rushing everywhere and shouting instructions to each other. Meetings were taking place all round the agency. Instead of the normal quota of ten employees we were up to forty-five ringers that day. The phone kept ringing off the hook – as I had instructed one of the secretaries to ring through to the switchboard every few seconds. The usual open plan space was divided into different departments by blue partitioning, what appeared to be palm trees, and the huge hexagonal columns that we had overnight repainted as giant HB pencils. I explained that we were having a normal, busy day. Once Mr Newman was installed in the boardroom, we gave him a short slide presentation about the agency and with my accountant, Steve, I showed him our accounts for the last couple of years. As he turned to the first page in the booklet, a flash went off outside the boardroom window. I apologised. I told him that we had a casting session that day and that the office was full of models for that reason. Sipping on the wine, and with the flashlight going off every couple of minutes, he simply could not concentrate on the task in hand. He quickly dispensed with the accounts (which incidentally were in order and made good reading) and said he wanted to see more of the agency itself. He was much more interested in the model photo-shoot that was taking place outside and he knew that, for every flash, he was missing yet another beautiful leggy model. In an instant he said he had satisfied himself that we were in good shape and, having finished with the financial figures, was outside the boardroom scrutinising the models' figures. He really enjoyed himself chatting up the girls and sipping his wine. He even tried directing once or twice, much to the amusement of the photographer, who was a friendly supplier who had set up the fictitious shoot. He stayed for about two hours and when (coincidentally!) the model shoot had finished and after the commissionaire had saluted him again, we had him chauffeur-driven back to his offices in the Strand. He reported back to the BYPS management team that we were exactly what they were looking for in an agency: vibrant, imaginative, and solvent. That afternoon, as soon as he had gone, I gave the all clear in the agency. The removal lorries arrived. They took away the plants, paintings, and the partitioning, as well as the leather sofas and other sundry furniture we had hired. The commissionaire went back to his agency and my cast of thousands all retired to the pub, where I joined them soon-after to buy them their well earned free drinks. The set-up cost us £5000 that afternoon, but it was worth every penny for the glowing report Mr Newman gave us. Then, a couple of days later we had a surprise telephone call from a mobile phone. It was the Marketing Director of BYPS. He happened to be in the vicinity so he thought he would just pop in and see our set-up for himself. He was ten minutes away from Soho Square. In an instant, I rushed over to our production department. We had invested in the best Apple Macintosh desktop publishing equipment. I had a very large, bold sign made instantly that read, "HOOK ADVERTISING is surprised to welcome MIKE BOWERMAN, the Marketing Director of BYPS", and we placed it on a large easel in the corridor near the entrance. As he walked down the long corridor to our offices, it was the only thing he could see. Mike was amazed by our speed of reaction. With just a few people in the agency that day, I had to explain that he had decided to pop in on a day when most of our staff were out on business. He said he had received a glowing report from Mr Newman and that we had passed our examination with flying colours. After that day we knew that we had the account in the bag and, as soon as we had signed the lucrative BYPS contract, we rapidly geared up the agency, both in personnel and equipment, so Mr Newman's agency illusion was no longer just a fantasy.

CHAPTER 32

Life's A Beach

As Hook Advertising flourished, I decided to throw a summer party for our clients, suppliers and friends. We had an alley beside our offices where we parked our cars. Our offices were open plan and opened directly onto it. It was about ten cars long by three deep. We removed all the cars and, having clad the floor of the alley in black polythene bags, we brought in trucks full of sand and covered the concrete with it to a couple of feet high. Then we covered the wall at the back with hoarding sized (20 feet by 10 feet) posters of exotic locations, Bacardi advertisements, sun-drenched beaches and sun cream advertisements. We dug small swimming pools into the sand, and lined them with inflatable paddling pools full of cold water and cans of beer. We brought in entertainers, limbo-dancers, fire-eaters and 10 page three girls, clad in bikinis, to act as waitresses for the evening. The guests were under strict orders that they had to wear beachwear or they would not be admitted to the party. Making everybody wear beachwear turned out to be a great leveller. Anyone who wanted to talk business had to enter a stretched limousine we had provided and it would take them slowly around Soho Square and its environs. Then we partied all night. We held the parties on two consecutive summers and they were a terrific success and easily paid for themselves in terms of the goodwill they generated amongst the guests.

CHAPTER 33

Seven Of The Best

During the early years of Hook's contract with the BYPS Consortium, we enjoyed a truly special relationship. We worked hard and we played even harder. Personal friendships and relationships were forged that still endure today. On one occasion, they challenged us to a football match. BYPS had geared up very quickly, and had employed a very dynamic, young, good looking sales force to try to snatch the initiative from their other three competitors. They were full of vigour and ambition, not just for themselves but for their company. The gauntlet was thrown down. Mike Kulezich, the Sales Manager, promised us that if we could scrape a football team together then BYPS would thrash us. The subject of the football match was the last item on our board meeting agenda. I knew that Mike had a strong bunch of players and I'd heard that he was planning to bring in a few ringers from other suppliers and contacts. I knew that we would struggle to put together a fit team from my artistic employees who prided themselves on being lovers rather than fighters. It was going to be no contest. Mike and his team were all mad-keen Manchester United supporters, so I told my fellow directors that the only thing we could do to prevent humiliation was to bring in a ringer ourselves. The match took place in the evening, at the Cambridge City Football Club ground which was directly behind the BYPS offices. I told BYPS that I would not be there in time for kick-off and to start without me. Mike had kitted out BYPS in the colours of Brazil to inspire them further – he and I had recently returned from the Italia 90 World Cup where we had followed the fortunes of Brazil – and the Hook team played in all white with the "HOOK" logo emblazoned on the chest. I pulled my Jaguar XJS into the car park twenty minutes after kick-off and sneaked into the dressing room. One of my players was jogging along the touchline and returning every couple of minutes to swill some of his pint of lager. It was time to make my substitution! I told the linesman, who called out to the referee and he stopped the game. Everyone on the field stopped and looked towards the dressing room. George Best, yes *the* George Best, emerged from the tunnel. He was kitted out in Hook's strip and slowly approached the touchline. Everyone on the pitch did a double take. My lager-swilling employee dropped his pint.

George Best makes a surprise
appearance for Hook – Photo from Mike Kulezich

Mike came over and shook George Best's hand. Then his entire team did the same. The game was held up for ten minutes. George Best was in good physical shape and both teams were mesmerised by his silky skills and awed by the fact that a football legend of his stature was on the park. He was a joy to watch. I had told only my fellow directors who my ringer was. Although the rendezvous to pick George and his partner was a pub, he had not touched a drop of alcohol and did not drink when the match was finished. George Best was candid, in the privacy of my car, about his various problems. He was charming. He stayed with us all evening; clearly enjoying himself despite drinking just tonic water, and took on (and beat) all-comers from both BYPS and Hook at pool – one-handed. At the end of the evening we sent him back to London in a chauffeur driven limousine. I paid him his fee in cash. He cost us £500. Oh and yes despite having George Best in the team, Hook lost 7-0. The tabloid newspapers covered the event the following day – the coverage was extensive, the publicity only did us good. Much has been written and said about George Best, especially since his untimely death. That night he was the perfect gentleman and professional.

CHAPTER 34

The Full Monte

In the early days of our contract, the Barclays Philips Shell Consortium (BYPS) swamped the agency with work and money. They were still recruiting sales people and could not afford to lose ground on their competition in persuading "site-providers for their transmitters" to sign up to their network. So the directors of Hook were teamed up with representatives of BYPS to run around the country and set up the deals. The schedule was a crazy one, and we would do several presentations a day of the marketing plans and leave the contract for the BYPS representative to agree terms. Very simply, a site provider, say Barclays Bank, who had high street branches around the country, would agree exclusively to install BYPS Rabbit transmitters in exchange for a rental fee. Thus the network was created. Our competitors were called "Zonefone", "Phonepoint", and "Callpoint", so our Rabbit idea stuck out like a sore thumb in marketing terms. It was far more memorable and creative, and indeed fun. The BYPS board of directors was determined to do everything more extravagantly than their competitors, so when we advised them that we should invite the main site providers to a secret launch of the brand, we had no problem in convincing them that it should take place in Monte Carlo in Monaco. To my delight, a party of four of us travelled over to the principality on a scouting trip. We were flown from the airport in a helicopter and I will never forget flying low to the seashore and over the bay into Monte Carlo itself. After a couple of days sunning ourselves and making the necessary arrangements, we agreed to hold the event there. We flew in our 80 guests on a specially chartered jet and booked them into the Loews Hotel, where that evening, in a full black tie event, we gave them a presentation of our marketing strategy, which, of course, ended in a magician pulling a rabbit out of a hat. This was followed by a cabaret show in the style of the Folies Bergeres and afterwards, a lavish dinner and a night in the casino. The following day we flew the tired, but satisfied and now fully signed-up, guests back to a cold dreary Heathrow. They were all clutching a cuddly rabbit with our inverted "R" logo on it. In 1990 the whole event had cost in excess of £100,000 but in terms of goodwill created for years to come, it was well worth it.

CHAPTER 35

Madness and "Pendulum Syndrome".

I have suffered from "manic depression" for almost twenty years now, although I have been in control of the illness for the last six years. The term "manic depression" is a misleading one; clouding public understanding and perception. The public sees the word "manic" as an adjective describing a severe form of depression. As Chairman of the Manic Depression Fellowship, I once gave a radio interview with the late Spike Milligan, who was then patron of the charity, where he emphasised to the interviewer that "when you're really, really depressed, you're manically depressed". I put him right and emphasised the dramatic difference in the high mood swings or "mania" and how they are followed by the deep and then clinical depression. In my experience, "mania" has inexorably been followed by deep depression. The word "manic" is also utterly destructive to our cause as it is the nearest word in the English language to the word "maniac" and the stigma attached to that word attaches itself to us in the very first utterance of the name of the illness. Thus, as a marketing man, I believe that the illness should be given a less emotive name such as "Pendulum Syndrome" or "P.S" for short. My first encounter with madness and manic-depressive psychosis took place on the morning of May 24th 1988, exactly 10 years to the time I had lost my arm. I have always celebrated May 24th as the anniversary of losing my arm, as survival rather than death and to this day I anticipate and watch out for coincidental events that mark the anniversary. My wife, Helen, unwittingly chose to break the news to me that she was pregnant with our first child on that day. It was as if a rocket had gone off inside me. I had the most astonishing rush of adrenalin. My joy was intense and I thanked God for, as I saw it, having given me my right arm back. I kept the intense joy to myself and drove to Waterloo station in my Lotus and dressed in a business suit where I gathered together a group of hungry tramps and treated them to a full English breakfast. It just seemed like the Christian thing to do. It was also outside my normal life and the scrutiny of others. Nobody who worked with me saw me do it and there was nobody there to approve or disapprove. Rapidly – although imperceptibly for me – my mood got more exhilarated, and within a couple of months I travelled to Teesside for my sister, Vanessa's, wedding to Dave. I was getting "high" for the first time. Although I had studied various languages at school and university, I believed that I could read and understand any language. I believed I had been divinely inspired and that I was slowly but surely turning into the Messiah. This has been a regular occurrence in my manic episodes, although when it happens I refuse to actually claim to be the Messiah because, after all, Jesus is said to have kept the fact that he was the Messiah a secret. I found hungry people and fed them and went into pubs where I was not known and bought everybody in the pub a drink. I believed that I was the life and soul of any gathering I went to, full of wit and charisma. I also believed that I was acquiring the strength and super powers of the heroes from the Marvel and DC comics. Indeed I identified with the heroes from all the myths and legends I had ever read. I thought it was my "calling" to save the world. The reality is that when a sufferer of "manic depressive" illness, which is fashionably known as "bipolar disorder" (a term that has come from the United States), is going through the high phase of their illness, his/her generosity knows no bounds. Therefore, you attract all kinds of people who are happy to relieve you of your cash. As I was working in the advertising industry and was particularly successful, I always had access to that cash and was used to spending and dealing in large amounts of money in running my business. I was used to the grand gestures and costs of the advertising business, and was oblivious to the fact that my actions were more and more grandiose. Couple that with the fact that I felt it my Christian duty to help people less fortunate than myself I became a target for every tramp, prostitute, drug addict or alcoholic who needed to be saved. As the psychosis deepens, there is a stripping away of self-restraint with regard to what is considered socially acceptable behaviour.

CHAPTER 36

Some Highs And Lows

For all that my mental illness has dogged and destroyed aspects of my life, there are some moments of madness that deserve to be recorded for posterity.

On one occasion, my mind had started to race, and I felt the need to escape from the rat race existence that I was leading in the advertising world. I took off, and decided to visit the monks at Pluscarden Priory in Elgin for a retreat. I didn't tell anybody where I was going, not even my wife Helen. With nothing but the clothes on my back and my wallet in my pocket, I caught a taxi to Kings Cross, where I generously tipped the driver. I jumped on the next train and purchased a first class ticket. I was joined by a smartly dressed businessman in his late fifties. I quickly engaged him in conversation. He turned out to be a senior executive from Rolls Royce and he was writing a speech for a conference on health and safety at work. I volunteered to him the benefit of my practical experience in the matter and he used it in his speech. The journey flew by. I arrived in Aberdeen and made my way to the monastery in a taxi. They were pleased to see me arrive but even more pleased to see me leave. The mania was upon me. Instead of experiencing a place of solitude for contemplation and prayer (as indeed Superman had to retreat to, in his fortress of solitude in the North Pole), I felt caught in a trap where the monks were governed by a bell that would spell out the rest of their lives; caught forever in a rat run that led to nowhere but the grave. When you're "high" you don't feel the need to eat regular "square" meals at set intervals. You are a "survivor" living on whatever fate throws in your direction. The monks were living the same life they had been living ten years earlier, trapped for life in a time warp. I had to free them from this slumber and free them from the routine where the bell governed their lives. I saw them as Pavlov's dogs; salivating when the bell rang at meal times. I had to save them from themselves. There was only one solution. While they were at prayer, I sneaked round their cells and changed the times on all their alarm clocks so that the next day they would all have their body clocks out of kilter, just like mine. They told me later that I had had the desired effect and they didn't appreciate it. Having "saved" the monks, I embraced Father Camillus who clearly recognised that I was not myself and he ordered me a taxi and I headed back to Aberdeen. Another effect of being "high", is that you just can't sleep. All your senses are finely and acutely heightened and sharpened, food tastes better – even sex seems better. I arrived at Aberdeen airport having missed the last plane to Teesside. I was going to return to my parents' house. For reasons beyond my comprehension, I seem to have an instinct that makes me home back to my parents' house in Teesside. As there were no planes back to Teesside I booked into a hotel and resolved to catch a plane the following day. However when the mania takes over I get more and more driven, so I discarded my suit in favour of a pair of beach shorts and a T-shirt and went back to Aberdeen Airport in the middle of the night. I then chartered an airplane to take me to Teesside, paying the £7000 fee on my American Express card. I remember sitting in the front of the aircraft chatting interminably with the pilot, who just thought I was an eccentric millionaire. As I stared out into the stars, I fully expected to be beamed up to the Star Ship Enterprise at any moment. When I arrived at Teesside Airport, my very dear friend, Duncan Walker, met me, accompanied by one of my employees, Mark. I had been pitching an advertising campaign idea of mine to Hertz hire cars based on changing the lyrics of the famous ballad "Love hurts, love scars" to "Love Hertz, loves cars" and had persuaded Hertz to hire me a brand new Mercedes Benz 420SL Convertible, and have it delivered from Newcastle to Teesside Airport. Outlandish and grandiose though my ideas and actions may be when I am "high", I am fully functional and entirely plausible to those people who do not know that I am ill, and, providing I can pay for my excesses, nobody seems to mind. Those nearest and dearest to me had tracked me down to Teesside Airport. The three of us drove to my home village of Norton in the Merc. Once in the local pub "The Unicorn", I bought everyone in the pub a drink. Then we jumped in the car and, to the horror of my friends, I floored the accelerator and started overtaking everything in front of me on a two lane road. I was "Batman" driving the "Batmobile" in the film. My friend Duncan stayed calm, but Mark was terrified and eventually Duncan persuaded me to stop and let Mark out. We pulled over and Duncan grabbed the keys from the ignition. At this point we were stopped by a police car. They had been watching from a distance. Duncan persuaded the police to take me to North Tees Hospital psychiatric ward. I agreed, provided I could wear the policeman's peaked cap! Later that night, I was sectioned under the Mental Health Act and detained at the hospital.

CHAPTER 37

Madeira And South Africa

Manic depressive psychosis has struck me many times over the years. I became ill when I travelled to Madeira with my wife Helen and toddler twins, Caitlin and Rebecca. I remember Helen trying desperately to persuade me not to go to the beautiful volcanic island and, while I was there, she tried desperately hard to make me take my lithium carbonate medication, even crushing the tablets and dropping it in my tea. However, I would not listen, and Helen and the children eventually agreed to come with me. When we got there, we stayed in the most opulent hotel on the island and I hired a taxi driver, who owned a white Mercedes, to chauffeur us around throughout the period of our stay. I bought myself a jellabah and wandered around dressed in this costume with nothing else but a pair of swimming trunks at night. While Helen stayed behind and watched over the children, I would roam around the seedier bars and eat and drink traditional fare with the locals. One night I found myself at the lift that transported people down to the private beach of our hotel. The lift was at the top of a large cliff and was closed for the night. I was livid. "How dare they lock up a beach" I thought. I wanted to swim, so I took off my jellabah and started to climb, one-handed, down the cliff face. I thought I was Tarzan and I clung onto vines and ivy with my hand and my teeth as I descended barefoot down the cliff face. When I got to some twenty feet above the beach, I jumped into the bushes below. I was scratched and bruised, and for a minute I thought I had broken my ankle, but with the adrenalin pumping through me I was keen to get on with my swim. On my own private beach in the moonlight and under a canopy of stars, I removed my swimming trunks and swam naked in the sea. I swam on my back in the millpond water that was the private bay. The pain in my ankle slowly dissipated. Refreshed and liberated, I put on my trunks and climbed back up the cliff face. I remember the startled expressions on peoples face as, dressed in my jellabah, I appeared over the edge of the cliff. Helen called a doctor to the hotel but, apart from examining my bruises, there was little he could do to help me, and I was oblivious to and cruelly dismissive of Helen's concern for my mental state. I was sectioned upon my return to Britain.

CHAPTER 38

Morocco

On another occasion I rushed, headlong and manic, from London to escape the build up of pressure in my head. With the lack of sleep and the brain in overdrive, I endure intense headaches as ideas flood into my head and I simply can't stop talking. My company and I were in the latter stages of the High Court battle with Barclays and Hutchison that I will refer to later, and I had just finished compiling a 110 minute video documentary which set out our case, without prejudice, and contained video footage of our witnesses giving evidence to camera. I had spent weeks producing "Caveat Emptor" (let the buyer beware – A reference to Hutchison, whom I alleged had not done their homework when they thought they had bought the "Rabbit" copyright), and sent copies of the highly embarrassing programme to the respective Chairmen and Chief Executives of our opponents. I was convinced that the prospect of a general release of Caveat Emptor would bring our opponents to the negotiating table – especially Hutchison, who were on the verge of launching their new system "Orange". A private viewing of the video was enough to encourage the Chief Executive of Hutchison, Hans Snook, to travel from Bristol to London to meet me in a hotel just round the corner from our offices in Tottenham Court Road. However we did not reach agreement. I was elated, and becoming hypermanic as the pressure increased in my business dealings and I escaped once again and headed back up North to my parents' house, carrying only a small leather holdall with a few belongings in it. I jumped in a black cab and told the driver to take me to Teesside, some 250 miles. He was incredulous. I made a stop at a cash dispenser and paid the cabbie half the fare up front with a promise of the remainder as soon as we got to Teesside. I arrived at my parents' house in the early hours of the following morning. The network of people who recognise when I am ill had already started to talk to each other and my overnight disappearance had not gone unnoticed. When I arrived in Stockton-on-Tees, my father was waiting for me and cooked me a hearty breakfast of bacon and eggs. When you are hypermanic you feel either voraciously hungry or not at all. I devoured my breakfast. Although the social service net that closes in on me had been alerted, I was conscious that it would not catch me until later that morning so, as my parents said the Rosary upstairs in their bedroom, I escaped once more clutching my holdall. Where could I go to overcome this mania without being be captured and incarcerated in a terrible psychiatric ward? I had to escape. I walked to the end of the road and flagged down a taxi. I asked to be taken to Teesside airport but discovered that there were no flights until the early hours of the morning. When one is hypermanic one has no patience. I headed for the railway station and jumped on the first train that came by. I ended up at Manchester Airport. Once there, I could not get a flight, so I jumped in a taxi and ended up at the Piccadilly Hotel in Manchester, where I vowed to try and get some sleep in an executive suite. I used a false name and paid in cash so I couldn't be traced. I wrongly, as usual, figured that I could beat this bout of mania by myself. I luxuriated in the perfumed bath and hoped that my brain would switch off. I felt clean and refreshed and caught another taxi to a brothel that was situated on the outskirts of Manchester. It was advertised in the local newspaper as a sauna. I sat on a comfortable armchair in the foyer and watched as punters came and went. I remember, most vividly, four Orthodox Jews in full black costume and beards as they brought in one of their party for his initiation. I had sex with one of the girls and returned to the hotel. I still couldn't sleep. As soon as the shops opened that morning I found the nearest travel agent. I had no idea where I wanted to go but I was adamant that I wanted to go as quickly as possible. There was a poster on the wall for Brazil but that would take some organising. So I booked the first trip available that day from Manchester International Airport – a self-catering trip to Morocco in my own apartment. I had my passport with me. I was in

Agadir in Morocco that afternoon. Although I felt that I could now relax from my "pursuers", the first thing I did was to go down to the local bazaar and buy myself a more traditional Moroccan costume. I distanced myself from the other people on the trip and immediately installed myself amongst the locals, preferring to sit and drink mint tea. Because of my colour I blended in very well. The trouble was that I was hypermanic. I went to the seashore and ate freshly baked fish with the local fishermen. But I could not stop. I could not sleep. So, when night fell, I walked on the beach and gazed at the moon and the stars or swam naked in the sea. Then I would return to my apartment and bathe in perfumed oils and smother myself in Chanel Anteus shaving lotion. I quickly found the locals' own bars and clubs, discotheques and rapidly attracted the attention of the prostitutes and less savoury characters as I splashed the cash. I believed I was immortal and some kind of superstar. I still couldn't sleep. I was totally driven. I was completely oblivious to the trail of concern and consternation that I had left in my wake. Then, in a moment of clarity, I telephoned my solicitor in the UK and told him where I was. One of my friends from the SAFE (Struggle Against Financial Exploitation – I shall refer to SAFE later) organisation I set up to help people fight back at banks, was despatched to find me and bring me back. I had adopted the hairstyle of the Moroccan men and was making regular forays into the suburbs of Agadir. I became more and more frightened of the spiral roads that led at night like a descent into Hell. As I got further away from my apartment and more and more lost, my French was useless to me and all the Moroccans seemed the same to me. I dismantled the apartment looking for the secret exit that would take me straight back to my home in London. I stopped eating because I believed the food was poisoned and I would only trust Coca Cola to drink believing the blue logo of the, ever-present, Pepsi to be a sign of poison and, with my preoccupation with copyright, a copy of the original drink. Wherever I went, there were people trading counterfeit goods in the cash and barter system. This was copyright Hell! I had at least four different fake "Rolex" watches while I was in Morocco. Eventually my colleague from Britain turned up and had me interned in a "psychiatric hospital", while he returned to England to make arrangements for my return. The "hospital" was the worst institution I have ever been in. Its façade was white and ornate and strikingly beautiful, but once you got beyond the doctors' offices you went in to the first holding area at the rear. There, at meal times, men in blue warehouse coats tossed pieces of loaves of bread dipped in syrup for the men to pick up and eat. The dormitories were all turned upside down with a thick layer of black dust covering the upturned beds. They were overrun with cats and there were no lights, or glass in the windows. The most horrific part of the institution was the holding courtyard at the back. The place was full of black sand and dirt and the Arab inmates lay on top of each other – the detritus of Agadir. Nobody spoke as they were too wretched to talk. The only sound was subdued sobbing and wailing. It was as if someone had piled a group of filthy Arab vagrants up with a bulldozer. But, as I walked around the yard surveying the scene, I witnessed an image that will stay with me forever. I saw two naked youths with their faces buried in the sand and with their split backsides in the air for anyone who wanted to use and abuse them. I could do nothing to help them so I took them some water. My colleague returned for me the following week and I was brought back to Britain. When I was well enough to leave hospital, I had to face the fact that my wife no longer wanted me in the house. I was distraught at leaving her and my young children and rapidly sank into deep depression. But this depression had a reason for it. I was extremely sad.

CHAPTER 39

Crazy Behaviour And Clinical Depression

To the inexperienced onlooker, the manic high of someone suffering from bipolar illness can just seem like extremely high spirits. To me, it is a gradual and steep acceleration of my brain. As my mind races I become more and more clever with words, often thinking of the most brilliant ideas and slogans and copywriting when I am "flying". Sometimes, if I have the good fortune to remember to write things down, at a later date I can make a profit from them. However, a lack of sleep and the "cold turkey" experienced as I come off the medication I have cast aside brings on terrible headaches and feelings of withdrawal. I often hear of celebrities who have publicly announced that they are "manic depressives". However I believe that if the "sufferer" has the insight to go and discuss their symptoms with a doctor or psychiatrist then they are still in control and are not suffering from full-blown bipolar illness, where the only real action that can be taken is to section the patient and to incarcerate them for their good and the good of the community at large. Sectioning is the legal process, by which the State confines a mentally disturbed person to a mental hospital under the appropriate "section" of the Mental Health Act). An approved Social Worker coordinates the process and seeks the written medical recommendation of two doctors; one of whom is usually a psychiatrist. An ambulance is called to bring the patient to the hospital but sometimes police back up is required, as the patient is often reluctant to go. The process sets out to be a dignified one, but usually turns out to be a public spectacle with the inevitable attention that is attracted from neighbours and passers by. More often than not, the half naked patient is manhandled by police into the back of a police van in hand cuffs. The first effects of stigma are felt from the moment a patient is publicly detained, but there is currently no sanitised alternative way of dealing with it. In the early nineties I met many sufferers of bipolar illness as Chairman of the Manic Depression Fellowship, which is the self-help charity that specifically targets this illness. In those days, and indeed to a large extent still today, we experienced terrible stigma and suspicion. I remember inviting the ITV lunchtime news into my advertising agency for a news item about the illness, and I felt very proud that I had emphasised the sheer productivity and spark that went with the condition. Viewers were able to see articulate and engaging individuals openly discussing the illness for virtually the first time. I remember one of my clients, Iain Bowles, of the Japanese computer giant Fujitsu, telephoning me to say he had seen the item. He was already enlightened on the subject of manic depression, as are many top executives in business. Unbeknownst to me, my staff had been telling my clients that I was on holiday in Peru. Iain was pleased to hear I was OK and wanted to ensure that I was still working on the Fujitsu account. I have noticed over recent years that the illness gets lumped in with other types of depression. But for me, there has always been a progression through stability to mania and then down to depression. The highs have always been followed by the lows and never the other way round. To deny that I enjoy some aspects of my manic episodes would be to lie, but the recriminations and feelings of lack of self-worth and self esteem, which come from the blame that is heaped on the sufferer after a manic high, lead a natural progression into sadness, melancholy, depression, and eventually, clinical depression – where sometimes the only route out appears to be suicide. In our society, it is very difficult indeed to look people squarely in the eye when you have exhibited signs of instability, inherent weakness, and insanity. People coyly refer to "a breakdown" or simply avoid the issue completely. The medical profession don't really know what causes it to trigger. Some believe it to be passed in our genetic make up, whereas others believe it is caused by traumatic shock. I believe my own illness is triggered by extremes of emotion. I recall my reaction to my wife's news that she was pregnant and also the shock of watching the drama of 9/11 unfolding live on television. Other moments have triggered rockets inside me, and soon afterwards I have become manic.

In 1994 I travelled on SAFE business to South Africa. SAFE had created such a furore in the UK about the High Street banks that word of our protests, demonstrations and other activities was spreading. We received a call from a businessman in South Africa who had read about us in his local newspapers. He was having trouble with his bank, so he funded us to fly out to South Africa, to Durban, to help him. After a long flight, we arrived and were chauffeur driven to our hotel. There was no time to rest however, and we had contacted the various supervisory institutions in South Africa to let them know we were coming. Although I was conscious of the impression we had made in the UK, I was not aware of the sheer power and strength the SAFE reputation carried with it. Thus the following day, accompanied by the businessman and without an appointment, we marched into the headquarters of the bank in South Africa. I simply walked up to the reception and gave the woman my SAFE business card. Within five minutes, the lift came down from the top floor of the skyscraper office block. It was the Chairman of the bank. He wanted to see if he could sort out the problem. I was blown away by the instant reaction of fear and respect that clearly now preceded SAFE. The rocket of emotional adrenalin fired through my system. Within days I was hypermanic and needed to be brought back to England. On my return, I was hospitalised.

CHAPTER 40

Five Star Hotel

One time when I was experiencing a manic episode, I took off and ended up in Leicester Square. I was dressed in a pair of black Timberland boots that I had bought in San Francisco when I attended the 1994 World Cup to watch Brazil, blue jeans and a vivid, blue long-sleeved shirt. I was wearing my false arm with the stainless steel C-hook on it. I thought I was Captain Hook. I bought the entire bunch of yellow roses from a seller in the square and proceeded to hand them out for free to every pretty lady I met. The place was buzzing late into the night. Then I went to the Kentucky Fried Chicken, and bought several buckets of food which I took to the tramps who were squatting around the Square. Eventually, I found a whole group of squalid-looking, unshaven and dirty-faced vagrants under the entrance to the Empire ballroom. I introduced myself to them and invited Peter, a large, scar-faced skinhead, to help me carry the food and cola over to the group. We feasted on the Kentucky Fried Chicken and watched the world go by. Then I remembered there was a luxury five star hotel in the opposite side of the Square. I had been there for many business meetings in the past. I counted up my new-found friends. There were seventeen. I told them to wait for me to return – not as if they were going anywhere anyway – and I marched into the hotel. I put my platinum American Express Card behind the reception and booked them all into the hotel. Although the hotel management were a little disconcerted at first, they readily accepted their new guests, and I sent them off to their rooms to have a long bath. Clad in the towelling robes of the hotel, they all came up to the Penthouse Suite that I had picked for myself, with its four poster bed and separate entertaining rooms. That night they were royally treated, eating á la carte and enjoying fine wines. At my behest, they ordered new clothes which were brought to them by the hotel staff and luxuriated with manicures and pedicures. I remember that Peter wanted a new pair of jeans, a new white T-shirt and a new pair of Doc Martins boots. But the highlight for me, was the fun I had with three very attractive young escort girls who joined me at the hotel. Jaimie, Jenny and Honey – two blondes and a brunette. They were delighted to entertain me together on the four-poster bed. After we had finished our romp, I lay back naked, propped up with pillows, and was royally hand fed by the girls with Aberdeen Angus steak, with champagne and strawberries and cream. Yes there was lots of cream. I was a king...or in heaven, or at least that's what I thought. However, the hotel management were getting edgy about the increasing numbers of down-and-outs joining our throng and, as the other guests were complaining, they called the police. Two uniformed officers knocked on the door of my suite and my guests scattered in terror. I ordered the policemen out of my room, telling them they had no right to select my guests. In the melee that followed, one of the officers had his helmet knocked off. He was totally bald. I shouted at him, "Get out of my room baldy!" – candour is one of the symptoms of the unfettered hypermanic. Once he had cleared everybody from the suite and the hotel, he returned with his partner and, wagging his finger at me, retorted angrily, "Never, ever, ever call me baldy... stumpy!" – I burst out laughing. I had clearly touched a sore point. I immediately paid my bill and left the hotel. That afternoon, as my movements were tracked by my network of concerned family and friends, I was stopped by the police in Holborn. Panicked by vague reports that I was a "psychiatric patient", when they saw my hook, six of them formed two rows and raised their batons, screaming at me to get down on the ground, to the great alarm of passers by. I did this immediately, without resistance and was then subjected to excruciating pain as my arm and false arm and stump were yanked up behind my back and I was sat upon by four of the officers, firstly on the pavement and then in the back of their van. With a knee in my face and my nose squashed against the van's doorstop, I finally managed to explain how they could literally "disarm" me. With my hook removed, they eventually relaxed their grip. It was a terrifying experience for me, and probably for them. But their first impression was that I was a Captain Hook "maniac", wielding a hook. Thank goodness they didn't shoot me. On another occasion, I was thrown down the flight of stairs in my parents' home by an impatient policeman who did not like the way I had ridiculed his attempts to handcuff me before he realised that I was a one-armed man. I do, however, remember with fondness, one occasion when I was brought in by soldiers in Morocco when I was finally tracked down by my colleague. For a so-called 'third-world' country, they were the kindest and most gentle "policemen" I have ever encountered. They were pleasant, showed patience and were utterly un-fazed by their task. I was not frightened by them, nor they by me. Psychiatric patients are not mad dogs. We are very vulnerable; and in a society where one in four people will suffer from mental illness, British police officers should be better equipped both in education, training, and resources, so that they can avoid acting like Dirty Harry.

CHAPTER 41

Hospital Assault

A psychiatric hospital can be a dangerous place. The staff are fearful of the unpredictability of the patients, and the patients are fearful of the punitive powers of the staff as well as the potentially violent instability of the other patients. Until you have been on the ward for a few days and know who is who, the atmosphere has the potential for violence. On one occasion I was manic and was brought into a hospital in Surrey. I was escorted in by two police officers and I was wearing a Brazil football shirt, shorts and trainers. I was not wearing my false arm. I was elated and resigned to my latest incarceration. I was, as usual, very happy and very talkative. I was escorted into a room just off the main entrance to the ward while the authorities transferred me to the care and custody of the psychiatric unit. I was left in the care of a male trainee psychiatric nurse, who was clearly a bodybuilder and I remember he had "Popeye" arms in his tight white shirt. We later discovered that he had failed to pass the training to become a police officer. I was left on my own with this man. Meanwhile, outside the room, the policemen who had escorted me in were enjoying a cup of tea. I was impatient about the apparent hold-up. I stood up and indicated that I wanted to leave. Before I knew what had hit me, he had yanked my arm up behind my back and forced me to my knees. I protested, and he released his grip on me so I could take up my seat again. Perhaps twenty minutes later, I stood up again and said I wanted to go home. He yanked my arm up again behind my back and pushed his foot into the back of my knees, catapulting me to the floor. My stump hit the thinly carpeted concrete floor and I heard the small bone, that remains in my upper arm, crack. There was no way of breaking my fall, as my arm was behind my back, my face smashed to the ground. Then, gripping my head by my hair, the trainee psychiatric nurse twice smashed it face first into the ground before kneeling on the side of my head. I was deeply shocked and, to make him release his knee from the side of my head, I tried talking to him. Blood gushed from my nose and face. I told him I was a Middlesbrough supporter and he told me he was an Arsenal supporter, slowly relaxing his knee and allowing me to get up. I sat back in the plastic chair and tried to staunch the blood that was pouring from my nose. The consultant psychiatrist and a social worker came in. The psychiatrist was more concerned about who was going to clean the carpet, than about me. At that point, I realised that the account of a sane man was always going to be believed over that of a man who has been sectioned. The trainee psychiatric nurse said I had tripped and fallen over. I thought to myself that I had no human rights. The following day, my estranged wife Helen came in to see me and she was furious with the hospital administration. She also wrote down a witness statement from me. That night, as the door to the ward was unlocked, I escaped from the hospital and made my way over to my friend, Keith Whincup's, house. Before we went to bed that night, Keith photographed my bruised and battered face. When I was returned to the hospital they treated me with kid gloves. X-rays showed that my stump was fractured and I had to wait patiently for the bone to heal inside my arm. I could not wear my prosthetic arm during the months of healing, and I have never felt comfortable wearing the false arm since.

I was released from the hospital in due course and I reported the assault to the local police but, because it had taken place in a mental institution, they would not pursue it. Three years is the time allowed to take legal action in a medical dispute. In 1999, exactly three years to the date of the incident, I exacted my revenge against the hospital where the incident had taken place. I issued a writ for damages against the hospital in the Central London County Court. On the same day, four of my colleagues from SAFE and I turned up at the hospital. We were all dressed in business suits and carrying leaflets.

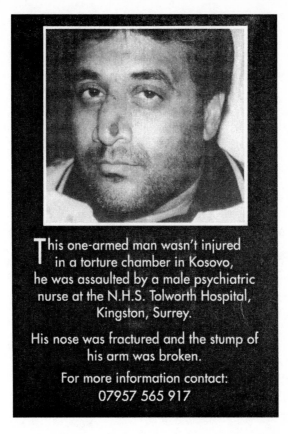

This one-armed man wasn't injured in a torture chamber in Kosovo, he was assaulted by a male psychiatric nurse at the N.H.S. Tolworth Hospital, Kingston, Surrey.

His nose was fractured and the stump of his arm was broken.

For more information contact:
07957 565 917

Going public in a medical dispute – Photo Steve Gale

The black and white A5 leaflets featured the photographs of my battered face that Keith had taken the night after the incident. The headline on the leaflet read, "This assault didn't happen in a torture chamber in Kosovo, it happened in a hospital in Surrey". There was a telephone number for more information. Like five gunfighters, we walked across the grounds of the hospital and onto the wards; distributing the leaflets to all and sundry. Even the security guards of the hospital gave us their blessing when they knew what had occurred. Then we went on the ward itself, where the incident had

115

occurred, and handed them to the patients who were in there at the time. I recognised some of the faces. Some of them thought we were lawyers who had come to prosecute their own human rights. Their faces lit up with hope when they read the leaflets. Having completed our leafleting, my colleagues and I were finally persuaded to leave by the ward staff, some of whom were in agreement with the protest and others who were horrified at our actions. We then retired to the local pub, where I held a press conference with the local newspapers and gave them the colour photographs of my battered face. We then made our way to Westminster where some 20 SAFE members handed out more leaflets outside the Department of Health.

Outside the Department of Health in Whitehall – Photo Steve Gale

These contained more true stories about physical abuse at the hands of psychiatric institutions. We set up a photographic opportunity of a man in a straightjacket being beaten by a man in a white coat, although only the Independent newspaper featured it. The employees of the Department of Health at Richmond House were very sympathetic on the whole but we did have the odd, very hostile, response. The story spread like wildfire around the area and made the front page of the main Surrey newspaper. It followed me back up to the North-east where I was interviewed for all the regional television news programmes. The following week, I returned to London to have a face-to-face meeting with the Chief Executive of the Trust where the incident had taken place. He was embarrassed and most apologetic. This time, I was dressed in a business suit and was treated with the utmost respect. One week later, the Trust settled the legal action for £8000 to avoid further embarrassment. The trainee psychiatric nurse was dismissed within two weeks of the incident, as his temperament was not suited to the work. My actions needed to be extreme because mental health institutions have an almost divine right to be believed in these situations, because their charges are mentally ill and apparently do not have the right to be believed in the same way someone 'sane' does.

CHAPTER 42

Squandering Money

When it comes to upsetting people, it is when I squander money when I am high that offends them most. With no concept of budget in their head, the manic-depressive is only limited by the extent of his resources and resourcefulness. People, generally, do not like to see money wasted but friends become very angry and jealous when they see the money being spent on total strangers. When I've been high, I have literally burned many a £20 pound note in an ashtray just to upset the people around me. Why couldn't I have given it to them they ask. On one occasion, at Gatwick Airport, I was standing on a balcony overlooking a long line of frustrated travellers who were delayed in checking in. It seemed like the most obvious thing in the world to lighten their load by tossing a sheaf of crisp ten pound notes off the balcony that floated like confetti all around. People abandoned the queue to grab the money as it floated through the air and all round them. I witnessed their reaction and disappeared quickly from the scene. I estimate that I threw away £500 but it was grossly exaggerated in the telling of the tale by my friends who witnessed it, as time went by.

On another occasion, I was sectioned after giving away £5000 worth of F.A. Cup tickets to kids. I had long been unhappy about the ticket prices at my beloved Middlesbrough Football Club. So, high as a kite, I arrived at the ticket office the day before Boro were due to play Blackburn in the F.A. Cup. I handed my credit cards over the counter, as well as a bundle of cash, and told the woman behind the counter to give me tickets to the value of the cash and the limits of my credit cards. I even had a bag of gold jewellery that I had bought, and tried to trade it for more tickets. The Commercial Manager, Graham Fordy, was called down from his office but, as he knew me personally he was happy to sell me the tickets – about 200 of them – but Graham politely refused to accept my gold in payment for more. I then walked to the nearby McDonald's, and started handing the tickets out to kids and passers by. However, someone called the police and, suspecting that they were forged, they came to question me. However, I was committing no offence so they stayed until I had finished and then let me get on my way. The following day, I was hospitalised for my own safety. At the time I was angry but I was detained for several weeks and gradually started to see sense again. When I was in hospital, I received several thank you cards from people who had used the tickets and been to the game, as well as a few visitors who wanted to thank me in person.

CHAPTER 43

Sectioning, Hospitalisation And Depression

Over many years, and perhaps a dozen episodes of mania followed by sectioning and hospitalisation, I have realised that restraint and recuperation are the only ways that society can deal with people who suffer from my condition. I have also learned to regard bipolar disorder as an illness, and not something that is inherently a weakness in my character. I no longer blame myself for the onset of an episode and thus my self-esteem is no longer devastated when I become ill. I believe that the descent into clinical depression is entirely rational. The recriminations that follow a manic episode, are many and far reaching. I know that my devious and erratic behaviour upsets those who are dearest to me, and, my excesses that both financially and in grandiosity, come home to roost. Even after all these years, I still get embarrassed when I recount some of the stories that have happened. Fortunately for me, I have a wide spectrum of friends, and the guilt and the blame is, if not forgotten, quickly rationalised and stored away. The manic episode is usually an ordeal in itself and then to have to undergo the incarceration while you come to your senses, is indeed hard. In the confines of the psychiatric ward, pain is exaggerated by the boredom and feeling of uselessness. Emotions run high and low, with grown men and women bursting into tears or laughter. The bills keep on coming and, by this time, your newly found acquaintances are long gone. Talk of homelessness, halfway houses and irate neighbours deepens the sense of despair. But the deepest feeling is that of the stigma of being classed as a 'mental' or 'psychiatric patient'. While inside the psychiatric wards, various business associates used the opportunity to take financial advantage of me. Also, on every psychiatric ward I have been on, there are trained or untrained personnel who are uncaring and even sadistic.

Only once have I ever contemplated suicide. Following a manic episode in London, I returned to our large Georgian house that backed onto Richmond Park. I was enveloped in darkness and inertia had taken over. I suddenly found that I had no reason to live and then, following a row with my wife who was simply trying to stir me into action, I took a dose of sleeping pills. But even in this irrational clinical depression, I was frightened of the fact that, whereas I know what is in this world and this life, I was afraid that there might be a worse or no alternative existence afterwards. I took enough pills to knock me out so I could escape my reality temporarily, but not enough to remove me from it completely. I do not have the courage to kill myself. I woke up with a terrible hangover and was inspired back to health by the joy of my twin daughters.

If I could have chosen not to have the illness then I would have certainly preferred to live without it. It has ruined some of my best relationships and it has taken me years to build bridges with some of the people I have offended. It has always struck me as ridiculous, and indeed insane, that the first action of the hospital doctors, upon sectioning, is to give the patient a legal copy of the section they are being held under. The person is by virtue of the sectioning, "insane". So how on earth can they be expected to understand such a document? Mental health wards all over the world are under-funded and, in my experience, (with the exception of the private Priory Hospital in Roehampton) dingy and depressing places. The wards are full of people with all types of psychoses including alcohol and drug-related illnesses. The over-riding feeling on every ward I have ever been on is that of mutual fear. The patients fear the staff as well as each other, and it takes a long while before that suspicion is relieved. The staff have powers of restraint, where, if a patient is not toeing the line in any way, they can be overpowered often by as many as eight people, wrestled to the ground and injected in the most humiliating way. Then there is the penalty of the high-security ward (lock-up wards) and padded rooms for particularly badly behaved patients. Psychiatric wards are containment areas, where patients must submit to incarceration until they have agreed to take, and are compliant with, whatever is the latest medication. Some of the staff on the wards I have inhabited have been sadistic, whereas others have been deeply caring individuals. When I was sectioned and placed in a psychiatric hospital/asylum in Paris in 2000, I remember one hulking individual of a male nurse who would derive great pleasure out of hosing down the naked patients first thing in the morning. As well as me, there was a motley selection of different people of all ages who would simply whimper and weep and suffer his cruelty every day. The mood on the ward can be lightened by what may at first appear to be trivial luxuries. As I can usually afford it, even after my manic excesses, I try to engender harmony on the ward by treating every patient on the ward to a takeaway meal. On more than a few occasions, I have sent out for Chinese, Indian, Pizza and KFC on the same night. Organising it is usually like a military operation; we have a feast. It is amazing to witness the happiness that this brings, even to the most depressed of patients. Also, one time when I was in a lock–up ward in the hospital where I was assaulted, I brought in a hairdresser friend, Patricia Whincup, and she gave all the inmates a smart new hairstyle of their choosing. It was astonishing to witness the dignity return to the inmates of that ward. When you break your leg people can see the problem, but when it's a mental health problem, it is concealed and people speak about it in whispers. Mental illness is taboo; even more so than amputation. People hardly ever send "Get Well" cards to psychiatric patients. I have managed to stay free of manic depressive psychosis for the last six years. But, I must be vigilant. I make sure I take the prescribed medication at the right times and in the right doses. I drink coffee first thing in the morning and remind myself to take my tablets with a slogan of my own invention – "COFFEE AND TABLETS MAKES YOU FEEL FABULOUS" – it doesn't quite rhyme but it helps me remember. I also watch closely for any changes in my sleep patterns. I try to remain unemotional about events in the news and in my private life, and I have deliberately avoided creative work challenges that might send me into overdrive. I have stabilised my finances and, during my period of remission, have worked with lawyers to create and establish a financial trust that can hold me in check if I become ill again.

CHAPTER 44

The Manic Depression Fellowship

In the early nineties, my long-suffering wife Helen, pointed me in the direction of the Manic Depression Fellowship. The MDF is a self-help charity that has groups all round the country. I remember that we used to meet in Barnes, at the house of one of our fellow sufferers for a cup of tea, some biscuits and a chat. It was good to meet people who had suffered episodes of the illness and just talk about the condition and compare experiences. Just as I had once thought I was Jesus, I have met other people who had thought they were the prophet Mohammed, or women who thought they were the Virgin Mary. Stigma comes from ignorance and the Fellowship seeks to act as a focal point for all aspects of manic depression. There was one man who used to just turn up at the meeting and curl up under the grand piano. Nobody thought any the less of him. The Fellowship is for both the sufferers and their carers and has flourished over the years. It seeks to educate as well as to campaign, and is now funded by Lottery money. I became the Chairman of the Executive and Chairman of the charity for a short time while Spike Milligan was Patron of the MDF. I even persuaded the Fellowship, in my capacity as an advertising man, to run an advertisement that was used all round the country as a poster. The headline ran, "IF YOU, YOUR FAMILY, OR YOUR FRIENDS SUFFER FROM MANIC DEPRESSION YOU'D BE MAD NOT TO JOIN US". I would advise anyone suffering from the illness to go to their local group meetings or form groups in liaison with the Fellowship. Believe me, the more that is known about the condition, the less the ignorance and the fear and prejudice. One of the saddest parts of being in the Fellowship is having known people who, despite their best efforts to conquer the illness, have succumbed to the depressive side and have taken their own lives.

CHAPTER 45

David V Goliaths

Hook Advertising quickly grew from one man (me) and developed into a company with an £8 million turnover, employing some 43 people and we moved offices a couple of times before finding a home in Soho Square. We worked for a variety of clients, including the computer company Fujitsu of Japan and the German hair care company Schwarzkopf. Our biggest client by far was a consortium company called BYPS which we won in 1989. I had negotiated and drafted the five year advertising contract with the Barclays Philips Shell Consortium (BYPS) for the Rabbit telephone system and it was the main source of income for the agency with a £300,000 p.a. fee which was index linked, as well as a hefty commission on all work we undertook. The agency was buzzing for the first 18 months of the contract and the consortium required us to gear up the company. Then, at the end of 1990, as the parent companies became disenchanted with the time it was taking to launch the telepoint network, they threatened to withdraw. At their informal creditors' meeting we were owed £736,000 by the consortium and they would not give us their assurance that they would pay. I warned them that if Barclays Bank, Philips Electronics and Shell Ventures were to pull the rug without paying, that they would never hear the end of it. In the event, they sold the business to Hutchison Telecom (famous for the Orange brand) that was a subsidiary of a giant Hong Kong company called Hutchison Whampoa and owned by a billionaire called Li Ka Shing. Although the new owners eventually paid us what was owed, we suffered such a cash flow crisis that, we had to reduce our staff by almost fifty percent and we lost the goodwill of our suppliers and – quite rightly – unhappy employees who had to suffer salary cuts. Within weeks of the takeover, we received a letter from Hutchison asking us for an assignment of the copyright in the "Rabbit" logo that I had created myself. As I said earlier, that was to be the sign and name of the telephone system. In the judgement of myself and my partners and lawyers, Hutchison, who had already terminated the contracts of many other BYPS suppliers, were preparing to terminate ours. We flatly refused to sign over the copyright as we did not believe it was covered by the terms of the contract. Frantic stressful meetings with lawyers and barristers ensued and then we got a visit from Barclay's head office. Apparently Barclays were prepared to increase our overdraft from £150,000 to £400,000 if we were prepared to put our houses on the line. If we accepted, we would not be able to consider Hutchison as a client and we would have to sign a confidentiality agreement preventing us from ever criticising Barclays and the other members of the Consortium. Repayment of the new overdraft was to be on demand. We refused and took the matters to our lawyers. In September 1991, Hutchison severed the contract with Hook and sued Hook Advertising and me in the High Court for an assignment of the copyright. We, in turn, sued Barclays, Philips, Shell, and Hutchison for various breaches of contract and for severing the agreement. Barclays withdrew Hook's banking facilities and sued us personally in the High Court for repayment. We stopped trading. Our opponents clearly felt that we would simply die under the financial weight of such opposition. However, they had underestimated our resolve and our resourcefulness and four years of litigation and attrition were to follow.

CHAPTER 46

The Bouncing Cheque

As Barclays tightened their grip on our banking facilities, our creditors started to feel the squeeze. Their cheques started to bounce and fearing the worst, they were polite but understandably angry. We issued them with new cheques but the bank was honouring some and bouncing others at random, and then charging us extra fees and charges for the privilege. Years of goodwill were disappearing down the drain and we discovered that extra charges were being applied for cheques that were represented. Also, some of our direct debits for our employees' wages were being dishonoured and rumours were rife, both in and out of the agency, about whether we were simply going bust. We could not keep the matter secret, so I decided to go on the attack with the bank. I needed to make a statement to inform our creditors that they should back off us while we tried to grapple with Barclays. They should not even attempt to bank our cheques or expect us to issue them with payment until the dispute was resolved one way or the other. I was aware that, in law, you may literally write a cheque on anything; so I contacted a glamour model agency to hire a Page 3 girl. I don't know whether the girl we used had ever been on Page 3 but she certainly had the necessary assets to carry off the job. I explained the nature of the job to the model agency and they were happy to help, as we had used them in the past for other work. Time was of the essence because we had to stop the rot as quickly as possible. She arrived the following morning and was accompanied by two make up artists and several of her friends. We took her into the boardroom for some privacy, and she perched on the boardroom table while her two girlfriends made up her face and then body-painted a copy of a Barclays cheque across and directly onto her bare and ample breasts.

SORRY MA'AM, YOUR CHEQUE HAS BOUNCED

● INTEREST rates shot up yesterday when stunna Rebecca Woolley walked into a bank and presented a cheque — written across her boobs.

● Rebecca, 19, peeled off her mac to reveal an order for £4,049.06 made payable to the BARER.

● Advertising boss Chris Joseph, 33, who tried to cash the cheque to publicise a court battle with Barclays, demanded to see the manager.

● But Nick Bates, boss at Barclays in Bishopsgate, London, took one look at the cheque across Rebecca's chest (bank code 340-24-34) and said: "I'm sorry but it would only bounce."

CASHPOINT: Chris signs the cheque   FLASHPOINT: Rebecca peels off

The bouncing cheque – Photo
reproduced by kind permission of Sport Newspapers Ltd.

The whole process took a couple of hours. We made out the cheque to one of our most loyal suppliers and, with quivering hand, I signed it. The model was wearing a dress that could be hitched down in an instant. I remember we had taken advice both from our lawyers and accountants as to the minimum detail necessary to make the cheque legal. Our cheque needed to be photographed and seen in the tabloids so we were quite accurate. We all jumped in a taxi and, accompanied by the tabloid press who I had tipped off, hotfooted it down to Barclay's Business Centre in Shoreditch, which was the home of our bank accounts. We entered the bank and hovered around in the foyer to sort out final stage directions. Accompanied by our friendly supplier and a number of photographers and journalists, I approached one of the windows and told them I wanted to present a cheque. In a flash, the model pulled down her dress and revealed the cheque. The woman behind the counter reacted quickly. She hit a panic button and, fearing a robbery, all the shutters, except hers, were rapidly slammed down tight shut. The other bank customers were both shocked and amused by our antics and just stood and watched. Having regained her composure, the bank clerk phoned upstairs for instructions. She directed us up the escalators to the office suite upstairs. I had not realised until that moment how powerful that and the stunts I would dream up in the future actually were. I headed the party, so I marched into the business suite and, with the throng that had increased by several more bystanders, simply stood and said nothing for a few moments. There were several business managers servicing that one business centre and they were all present, with the exception of our own manager who was out on a long lunch. After a couple of minutes of silence one of the managers spoke to us. He was standing about twenty feet away and his voice was shrill and nervous, as if there was a hold up in progress. He backed off from our group as if he were in some physical danger and, with his other managers forming a tight group behind him, he explained that the Hook bank manager was not around, but that they had paged him to come back from his meeting. It was a bizarre sight; since the offices were open-plan, everyone was interested in what was going on and all the bank's employees, both male and female, were standing silently on their desks watching the spectacle. Wolf-whistles pierced the air, followed by jeers of approval. The whole business centre had come to a standstill. This only emboldened the glamour model who postured and posed for the cameras and the bank clerks. The bank managers shouted at their employees to get on with their work, but they took no notice. Eventually, we all agreed to go into a plush meeting room and wait. Minutes later, Hook's manager arrived. During the years of our success we had enjoyed an excellent relationship. He had enjoyed our hospitality on many occasions – I remember taking him, as our guest, to the Olympic Gallery hospitality suite at the old Wembley Stadium to watch the Manchester United v Crystal Palace Cup Final in 1990. However, since the dispute had arisen, he had become a pawn in the bigger Barclays picture. He was briefed by his fellow bank managers before coming in to see us, and had consulted his head office. He was calm and cool and informed me that Barclays would not honour the cheque. However, to give him his due, he joined in with the spirit of the occasion, and joked with us that he would personally love to pay the cheque as he would get to keep it in his vaults for twelve years and take it out every now and again to handle it! I was conscious of the presence of the journalists who were looking for the right headline. We refused to leave until the manager said the immortal words "Sorry, I'm going to have to bounce your cheque". The following day, several of the tabloids and other media covered the story. We had our pictures and indeed our headline. We wrote a letter and enclosed copies of the "bouncing cheque" articles to all of our creditors. It was finally out in the open – we were officially in dispute with Barclays, one of the biggest banks in the world and moreover claiming to be our biggest secured creditor; and the best thing our unsecured creditors could do was sit back and wait – the message was high profile, embarrassing and humorous and within the law. That day Hook Advertising stopped trading and started fighting back.

CHAPTER 47

SAFE logo – copyright Chris Joseph

SAFE Struggle Against Financial Exploitation

Anyone who has ever used either the Civil or Crown Courts will know what a tortuous and indeed torturous, process it can be. A lengthy endless and expensive paper-trail and mire of claims, counterclaims, and preliminary proceedings that seem to go on forever before a full trial takes place with its many and varied procedures. The High Court building in the Strand is an awe-inspiring place, that strikes fear into the hearts of even the strongest of those seeking justice. Most cases never reach trial, with poorer protagonists simply not able to proceed or being too frightened to go down that route in the first place. Most cases are settled somewhere along the line or the plaintiffs lack the will or the means to be able to bring them in the first instance.

I decided that we could either die out slowly and quietly, or, make as much noise as we could. I also figured that these huge corporations could live without the embarrassment. As public companies, they cannot let their public image become tarnished, so I decided to take the game to them and fight them on many different fronts. I wrote a letter of complaint to Sir John Quinton, then the Chairman of Barclays Bank. He did not reply, so I had the letter blown up onto a giant mobile billboard and then had it parked outside Barclay's Headquarters. My actions were featured in the *Sunday Times* newspaper and I was contacted by a number of people, from all professions, who were experiencing problems with their banks. We convened a meeting in Hook's boardroom and decided to collaborate by forming an umbrella organisation for victims of financial institutions. I set up a company limited by guarantee of which I was Chairman and we named it SAFE – Struggle Against Financial Exploitation. Within a few days, there were several mobile billboards travelling round London, all bearing tales of woe from Barclay's customers. SAFE's membership grew and grew, and we organised publicity stunts to draw attention to the plight of small business customers who were being treated badly by their banks and other financial institutions. We designed and produced satirical T-shirts, parodying the logos and advertising slogans of the high street banks. BARSTARDS BANK – YOU'RE WORSE OFF TALKING TO BASTARDS, – NATZI WEST – THE ACHTUNG BANK, LLOOTS BANK – THE THOROUGHBAD BANK.

Protest t-shirts – designed by chris Joseph

As the court cases rumbled on, I bought a few shares in Barclays and attended their AGM with my Member of Parliament, Frank Cook, Labour MP for Stockton North. Frank Cook raised the matter in the House of Commons. We were quickly joined by an MP from the Conservative Party called William Powell, MP for Corby. Whenever they raised the issue in the House, they were covered by Parliamentary Privilege and their comments were reported in Hansard and could be quoted by journalists. As shareholders, we quizzed the Chairman about the number of companies or individuals who had been silenced from criticising Barclays using these special agreements. What started as a small thorn in the side for Barclays and the other companies, soon turned into a serious problem, as more and more journalists picked up and reported our various horror stories. Eventually our actions were reported in the financial press and featured on "World in Action" and the "Money Programme". The *Sunday Times* reported us as the second most high-profile membership protest organisation after Greenpeace. My initial protest using the billboard had attracted the attention of a new lawyer. Bruce Ross was a lawyer who was originally from New Zealand and he was excellent throughout the case, not bowing to the enormous pressure placed on him by the huge legal teams employed by our opponents. We would ensure that all our publicity stunts were legally checked before we did them because we knew that our opponents would pounce on any mistake we made. "The Companies Act" and "The Banking Act" became bedtime reading as we sought to flex the muscles of the single-share holding shareholder. We approached, and met, the Department of Trade and Industry and the Bank of England. When they ignored us or were deliberately unhelpful, we turned our sights on them for not fulfilling their supervisory roles. In 1993 having convened our own "Not the AGM" Barclays shareholders' meeting across the road from the Queen Elizabeth II Centre, we took 300 individual shareholding shareholders to the AGM of Barclays Bank. Some were armed with difficult questions for the under-fire board, while others were there just to vote against the resolutions. With all the information we had gathered, we published an A4 glossy magazine called "A Critical View of Barclays", which we distributed at the meeting. We asked searching questions about the bank's solvency and brought details of our allegations to the attention of the shareholders who were present. Indeed, for many months after that fiery AGM, we were contacted by numerous financial organisations seeking a copy of our different perspective on Barclays. We carried out a poll and discovered that Barclays was, at that time, the most hated of the high street banks. We presented them with a certificate – "WORST BANK IN BRITAIN" at their AGM and followed it up by sending them a vacuum cleaner with an invitation to "Clean up your act". We whipped up the small-business anger that existed towards the banks at that time and again, to coincide with their annual results we erected a billboard in the heart of Covent Garden and "hanged" a man in a business suit next to the slogan "CRUCIFIED BY BARCLAYS, WHILE THE BANK OF ENGLAND WASHES ITS HANDS".

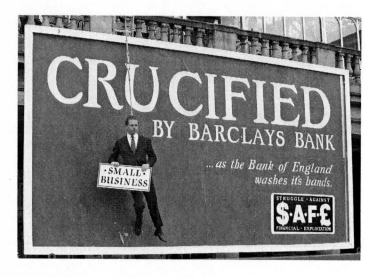

Living poster in Covent Garden to coincide with Barclays annual results. – Photo: Steve Gale

We may have mixed our metaphors, but our message was strong and unequivocal. The dramatic photo opportunity was the main story on ITV's "News at Ten" programme that night and eclipsed Barclay's results for that year.

After the AGMs we would drink champagne and eat the delicate canapés and sandwiches and mingle with our fellow shareholders and make the Barclays Directors uncomfortable by accosting them, quizzing them and asking them for private meetings which they found difficult to deny to their shareholders. I met Andrew Buxton, Chairman of Barclays and Martin Taylor, the Chief Executive, on many occasions but we failed to resolve the dispute. I also became a shareholder in Philips and Shell and turned up on my own at Shell's AGM on more than one occasion. I had meetings with the Chairman of Shell UK and the Chairman of Shell International. With each meeting came more titbits of information, and a gradual lifting of the corporate veil and a glimpse of what was behind the BYPS Consortium. I decided that Mr Li Ka Shing, the Hong Kong billionaire who owned Hutchison Whampoa, should not be immune to our attentions, so I took a series of press advertisements in the Hong Kong newspapers, directly addressing him and asking for talks.

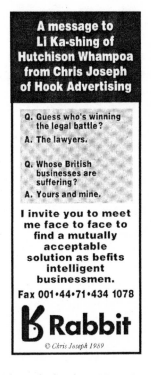

Taking the battle to Hong Kong

In a furious, and I believe considered letter from the top of Hutchison Whampoa, Hutchison's Chief Executive let slip that they had bought the BYPS company from Barclays and not Philips or Shell, so we released them from the legal actions. We used the letter as evidence in the High Court to show Barclay's direct culpability in the whole sorry saga. Also, we discovered that Barclays had insured Hutchison against any legal action involving the Rabbit logo.

CHAPTER 48

As Safe As The Bank Of England

The Bank of England has the task of supervising the conduct of banks under the Banking Act. We decided that they were not performing their duty, with the old boy network preferring to ignore any misconduct, and allowing the banks to supervise themselves. To this day the banks operate to the voluntary code of conduct we were instrumental in forcing them to adopt, and to demonstrate some accountability from the protests we made in the nineties. We decided as the Bank of England was their supervisor, we should turn our attention to them as well.

CHAPTER 49

The Goat

In the early nineties, Nick Leeson, the famous rogue trader brought down Barings Bank through misconduct and lack of proper supervision. In our document "A Critical View of Barclays", which we had distributed at the Barclays AGM the previous year, we had forecast that a rogue trader might bring down a bank. In the same document, we had published the response of Robin Leigh Pemberton, the former Governor of the Bank of England to a simple SAFE question "Q". Can you categorically confirm or deny that depositors' money is 'safe' in Barclays Bank? ". Pemberton replied "A". ...the fact that an institution is supervised by the Bank does not, of course, mean that the bank, in any way, guarantees its obligations". Cold comfort for depositors. It was astonishing how quickly the Bank of England, and a specially convened team headed by Andrew Buxton of Barclays' bank, attached blame to the individual. The lack of tangible supervision from the Bank of England and banks in general, who sometimes recklessly allowed their employees to take crazy risks with the hard earned money of their depositors, was replaced by a worldwide media witch hunt for Leeson. At SAFE, we decided to ensure that Leeson did not get all the blame. We turned up, en masse, at the Bank of England and led a tame ceremonial goat up the steps of its hallowed portals. The City of London police were present but decided not to intervene, as our protest was peaceful as usual.

Scapegoat protest outside the Bank of England – Photo: Steve Gale

The goat was wearing a specially designed shawl bearing the name of Nick Leeson. The security guards at the doors of the bank were on red alert as we mounted the steps. We were pursued by television cameras from the BBC and several photographers and reporters. When we got to the top step, Nick the Goat made a deposit and we attempted to enter the Bank of England. The famous Bank of England guards, resplendent in their pink top hats and tails, rushed and closed the doors with an almighty bang, pulling the huge bolts up to stop us from entering. It was a claim to fame that until that day, the doors to the Bank of England had always stayed open for business, even during the Blitz.

CHAPTER 50

The Islamic Bankers Convention

As SAFE was so high profile and had adopted a lawful and informed strategy, we were considered to be in "the loop" and invited to seminars and conferences. I went with one of my colleagues to a meeting of Islamic bankers. The conference was held in Leicester and there was a fee for the tickets. I must admit I had an ulterior motive. The then Governor of the Bank of England, Eddie George was the keynote speaker. My colleague and I installed ourselves at a table in the front row. There were about 150 delegates, including other governors from the Middle East etc and other economic experts. I will never forget the look on the face of Eddie George. He was at the top table, facing the delegates. As the conference started, he was sitting on the rostrum staring into a sea of brown faces and he noticed me looking intently at him. He was clearly disorientated, and had to double take and then look again to check on my brown face. I decided to help him out. I slowly but surely turned around my name sign that was on the table. It read "Chris Joseph, Chairman, SAFE". I could see the blood drain from his cheeks. His speech was about the stability of the Western model of banking, as exemplified by the British Banking system, and called for a greater interdependence between the western and eastern models of banking. He delivered it nervously, every now and then casting a watchful glance in our direction as I'm sure he was expecting some kind of publicity stunt. However, I waited for the question and answer session immediately afterwards and put up my hand. I asked him how he could seriously ask for an arranged marriage between eastern and western banking, when the Bank of England had failed utterly in its supervision of Barings and BCCI and others. I suggested that the more stable Eastern model of banking would find itself performing the role of a safety-net, over which the Western banks could perform their unregulated high wire acts. He was purple with rage. He was embarrassed that he was being quizzed in front of what he thought would be a passive and respectful audience. My comments were listened to and picked up by others in the audience, and, to my great amusement, a fuming Eddie George walked out of the meeting room, pursued by journalists and television cameras representing Middle Eastern television channels. He got into his chauffeur-driven limousine and drove away at great speed.

CHAPTER 51

300th Birthday Party

In 1994, the Bank of England celebrated 300 years since its formation. Governors of national banks from all round the world were invited to London to join in the celebrations. SAFE decided to follow suit. We researched the events that the Old Lady of Threadneedle Street was throwing for the governors, and discovered that one of the main events was a seminar and cocktail party at the Barbican.

Wealth Warning:
BANKING WITH BARCLAYS CAN SERIOUSLY DAMAGE YOUR WEALTH

$·A·F·£

S.A.F.E., 15 Adeline Place, Bedford Square, London WC1B 3AJ 0171-636 6601

SAFE protest leaflet – Photo Steve Gale

Four of us went to the seminar, which was held in a lecture theatre at the Barbican. We were dressed in tuxedos and carrying carrier bags, and at the end of the lecture simply joined the throng of guests and made our way into a large function room. We enjoyed their best champagne and canapés with the guests and handed them SAFE leaflets from our carrier bags, as well as a specially prepared letter addressed to Governors from all round the world. We shared a joke with the jovial representatives of their national banks and they were fascinated to hear our stories of the lack of supervision, of which we were spokesmen for the victims. Some of the governors wore national costume and, without exception, they were full of admiration for us having taken the trouble to bring matters of concern to their attention. We had been in the reception room for an hour and a half when, to my surprise, I turned around and physically bumped into Eddie George, the Governor of the Bank of England. He instantly took one of my leaflets and then asked me the dumbest of questions; "What are you doing here? Do you have an invitation?". I told him I did not and he rushed off to get a security guard.

A couple of minutes later, a beefy doorman had invited two of us to leave. He listened to what we had to say and, sympathising with our grievances, allowed us to place the leaflets strategically on coffee tables round the room so that the governors thought they were official leaflets and pick them up to read later at their convenience. We left our other two colleagues inside for another hour and stayed in touch with them by mobile phone from a nearby bar. Eventually we departed; a job well done and in a lawful and peaceful way. As usual, we reported our activities through the national newspapers and increased the pressure on all the relevant parties, not only to our own dispute, but also to others relating to SAFE members.

Barclays cost us an arm and a leg

Chris Joseph (hook) ran a successful small business (40 employees) until Barclays Bank cut off its banking facilities. Now they've admitted a massive blunder. They underpaid his business more than £43,000 interest. Barclays have apologised, but "unemployed people can't live on apologies" says Chris.

Ron Clifton's hopping mad. Even as he lay in hospital waiting to have his leg removed, his Barclays' manager was harassing him on the telephone. He was £10 over his limit ... who would pay if he popped his clog(s)?! Ron *does* want an apology, but Barclays seem to think they're better off *not* talking.

Chris and Ron are members of SAFE, an organisation that shows bank customers how to fight back against blunders and malpractice. SAFE needs your support, whether you want to become a member, make a donation, or simply add your voice to the growing campaign for bank reform. After all, *it's our money !* Whatever you do Chris and Ron say:

"Don't let the Barclays grind you down!"

STRUGGLE · AGAINST
$·A·F·£
FINANCIAL · EXPLOITATION

FOR MORE INFORMATION SEND A S.A.E. TO SAFE, 5 GREAT CHAPEL STREET, LONDON W1V 3AG

SAFE press advertisement – Photo Steve Gale

CHAPTER 52

A Man Named Sue

As Hutchison rolled out the new Rabbit system across the country, they placed their transmitters or base stations at prime locations, and displayed the Rabbit logo to identify to their customer base the location from where they could make a call. We decided to sue these companies too, as third party infringers of copyright and so I sued Barclays, Comet, Dixons, Currys, Boots, Trust House Forte, British Airports Authority and London Underground, as well as a number of other high profile companies. BAA chose to ignore the writ, so we entered judgement against them. Eventually, our third party writ was defeated in the High Court but behind the scenes we had caused a degree of panic with site providers demanding insurance against legal proceedings by us from Hutchison, if they were to display the Rabbit logo. I bought single shares in most of these companies and attended their AGMs to ask them embarrassing questions about copyright infringement.

CHAPTER 53

Clerical Error

As our case proceeded through the High Court, I realised that our opponents would seek to draw matters out, in the hope we would not survive the lengthy process. Thus I was constantly embarrassing them with publicity stunts so they would either settle or at least want to bring matters to the High Court more quickly. Barclays decided to try to force the situation by pursuing us personally over the outstanding overdrafts and debts of the company. They got judgement against us in the High Court for all the outstanding monies. I remember that day vividly. We were in despair. I went into a wine bar across from the High Court in the Strand and thought up a strategy with our lawyer, Bruce. I visited a company up in Oxford called Audit UK Ltd. They check for errors in bank accounts. A few hours later, we had discovered that Barclays had failed to pay Hook Advertising some £43,000 worth of interest on a high interest account, whilst wrongly charging extra interest on our overdraft. Armed with this new evidence, we meticulously and forensically reworked the figures, showing that Barclays had, in effect, committed trade libel by bouncing cheques for less than they owed us at the same time. Following yet another heated round in the High Court, Barclays refrained from using this route to stop us. They explained that it was a clerical error but the Judge was not prepared to listen to them, and threw them out. To coincide with their annual results, I arranged for a giant mobile billboard with their error on it to arrive at their HQ just as the Barclays Chairman was being interviewed by the Money Programme and News at Ten and then to do a week's tour of major UK cities.

Barclays' big mistake – Photo Steve Gale

CHAPTER 54

Crown Court

Hutchison meanwhile, complained to the Westminster City Council that Hook had breached the Trades Description Act. They hoped to secure a criminal prosecution against us, to bolster the credibility of their Civil Court actions and to provide them with yet another alleged breach of contract. After a dramatic week long hearing in front of a judge and jury at Southwark Crown Court, Hook was acquitted of all charges. The jury took less than ten minutes to reach its unanimous verdict and I'll never forget their smiling faces as they returned to their seats to give their decision. They could see what Hutchison's motives were and they were not prepared to allow it to happen. We dashed off afterwards for a champagne reception and the ordeal had only added steel to our resolve.

CHAPTER 55

The Rabbit Trial

The High Court trial over who owned the copyright in the Rabbit logo, was eventually heard in the Strand at the end of 1995. I had just been brought back from my horrendous experience in Morocco and was in deep clinical depression because I was no longer living with my family. The trial was delayed for a week to see if I would pull round and, eventually, I entered the witness box. As I was grilled thoroughly by their excellent barrister, Mark Platts-Mills QC, I found myself slowly but surely emerging from my deep depression. There is nowhere to hide in the High Court once you are in a witness box, and Mr Platts-Mills had me cross referencing my evidence and testimony between a number of different bundles of documents as he sought to trip me up and prove his case. As Mr Platts-Mills had recently been made a Queen's Counsel, we had to bring in our own QC and could not be directly represented by Richard Hacon, who was the expert on the case and had represented us throughout until the trial. In the event, the lady judge came up with a judgement that was delivered with the wisdom of Solomon. She found that we had effectively offered, and given the Rabbit logo to BYPS (Hutchison) in an unwritten "preliminary agreement" through our actions prior to the signing of the contract. However, the judgement confirmed once and for all, that an advertising agency is likely to own the copyright in the ideas it pitches in most cases, and is now used as the benchmark case for the advertising industry.

However, this left it open for us to pursue our claims against BYPS for unlawfully severing the contract and for the claims and counterclaims against Barclays. Once again, Hutchison tried to stop our case against them from proceeding by asking the High Court to order us to pay £40,000 into court for security against their prospective costs for continuing. The judge gave us the weekend to come up with the money, or we would be struck out. We rushed around crazed that weekend and managed to raise the cash. On the Monday morning, our barrister, Jonathan Crystal, who represented us superbly throughout both in formal and informal tactical advice, announced to the judge that we had paid the money into court. Our opponents immediately called for settlement talks and we entered into, what I found to be, a lengthy and very high pressure and stressful negotiations. We settled for a seven-figure sum that I am not allowed to disclose under the deeply paranoid terms of the agreement I eventually signed. Our opponents had never counted on our resolve or staying power. They had underestimated the lateral thinking, coordination and indeed sheer unpredictability of our strategy and actions, and their corporate machines could not keep up with the diversity of our unfettered creativity; after all we were an advertising agency run by a madman!

CHAPTER 56

Pies For Spies

I returned to live in the North-east of England at my parents' house. I was going through, what the medical people referred to as, a "revolving door" when it came to my mental illness, with recurring episodes of mania and hospitalisation, followed by depression. However, I remained productive. One day I switched on the television and watched with interest as former MI5 officer turned "whistleblower", David Shayler, was released from jail in Paris. He was accused, and later convicted, of breaching the Official Secrets Act. He was wearing a football shirt. It was the Argentina-style light blue and white striped second strip of my beloved Middlesbrough Football Club. I devised a plan with my butcher friend and fellow Boro supporter Martin Blackwell, to bake one of his famous pies with 007 in pastry on top for David and do a "pies for spies" promotion. The journalists loved it, coming up with their own slogans like "For your pies only" and "The pie who loved me". Very soon I was in touch with the human rights organisation Liberty, who were representing David, and then David rang me himself from Paris. I arranged to take a consignment of meat pies to Paris for David, who was effectively in exile and on the run from the British authorities. I arrived at Charles de Gaulles Airport in Paris sporting my Middlesbrough shirt and had arranged for David to be wearing his Boro shirt so that we would "recognise" each other. I was stunned at the attention our stunt had attracted with the world's media gathered to witness the handover. "Donnez-lui le gateau" shouted one reporter, who clearly had no real idea what was going on.

Pies for Spies – Photo: Chris Joseph

We did the honours for the cameras and the story went out all over the world. I had some private time with David and his girlfriend, Annie Machon, and I agreed to represent him, both to publicise him and hopefully keep him safe and also to act as his literary agent. At that time, he and Annie were very frightened that something sinister might happen to them and we moved furtively from café to café, keeping a constant eye out for anyone who was following or might be hiding behind a newspaper. Then David said he was just going back to their apartment and would be a short time. Annie and I waited for a long while before David came back. She was very concerned but I guessed he had got stuck in to the pies. I was right. David returned and said he had enjoyed a slice of turkey and ham pie with a glass of wine. When I flew back to England that night, I got caught up in the paranoia. I was approached by an old Orthodox Jew in full garb. I was about pull his false beard off when he quietly asked me for directions to the toilet. Over the months that followed, I made many more trips to Paris and acted as David's publicity agent in the UK. I remember taking him over a large bottle of Branston pickle which he said he could not get in France.

Bring out the Branston – Photo Bob Gaught

I liaised with the numerous journalists who wanted to speak to him, and produced a campaign called "PUBLIC FRIEND No. 1." for him and acted as his adviser, even buying him suits and ties and paying for his haircuts before he made an appearance. We figured that the more high profile he was, the safer he was. The first thing I did for him was set up a press conference with him talking directly to journalists by a live link-up to Paris. I was instrumental in persuading him to come back to England to face the music and set the date with him for his return.

CHAPTER 57

The Un-Crucified Spy

My colleagues from SAFE and I performed several publicity stunts to highlight David's plight. The Home Office sought to censor his novel "The Organisation" by advising would-be publishers that they may be publishing official secrets. I circulated the manuscript around a variety of publishers and, although they were keen to see it, they were too timid to take it any further. We decided to submit it to the Home Office for approval and a time and a date were set up for the handover of the script. Several of my SAFE colleagues in suits and dark sunglasses, turned up with me for the handover of the script to the government's solicitor. As we had indicated that the book was about spies, sex and football, we played football on the steps of the Home Office building while a delightful cancan dancer called Vicki, high-kicked her stuff for the cameras.

A pint in Paris – Photo Chris Joseph

We then organised a trip to Paris to coincide with David's third anniversary in exile. Four members of SAFE, Bob Gaught, Keith Whincup, Geoff Hobson, and I made the trip from London to Paris in a minibus. On board, we had a large full-size red crucifix which had been engineered by my friend Geoff (SAFE's props man). The "Cross" allowed a protester to stand comfortably on a platform while giving the appearance of being crucified.

Getting cross with Barclays Bank – Photo Steve Gale

We had used it in our anti-bank protests. It was engineered out of plastic drainpipes and, as such, was very lightweight. We travelled through using the Eurotunnel and drove to Paris. We met with David, although Annie was ill, and stayed overnight in a hotel, and following breakfast the next day we drove towards the British Embassy where David was to deliver a speech from the crucifix. We had notified the media as to our intentions, but unfortunately we were stopped by the French Intelligence service when we were only about 200 yards away from the British Embassy. A plain-clothes officer who we nicknamed "Inspector Clouseau", pulled us up in an unmarked car. We were surrounded by marked vehicles and as I explained our intentions (I was the only member of the group who could speak French), we were directed to pull over to the side of the road. It was a bizarre scene; a one armed man in a suit speaking to a French agent about crucifying a British spy. "Clouseau" told us that we could hold a demonstration but that he had received strict instructions that we could not erect the red crucifix "in the French Republic".

Outside the British Embassy – best laid plans – Photo Bob Gaught

We still had placards and Tony Blair masks that we eventually wore while David delivered his speech from the pavement outside the British Embassy. In true theatrical style, he turned up late for the crowd of waiting journalists riding a tandem. We got the coverage we had wanted but without the photos of David "crucified by the British government". The diminutive plain clothed "Clouseau" popped up wherever we were during that crazy afternoon. He never let us out of his sight but allowed us to get on with the protest. Eventually, after the demo was finished and David was giving interviews to individual journalists, we retired to a café and I explained the details of the allegations against David to "Clouseau". We said he was only doing his job and we made it clear we felt we had been treated properly. I arranged for David to autograph a small Union flag and we presented it to "Clouseau". He was delighted. He said he was due for retirement and in all his years he had never felt less threatened at a demonstration and he had certainly never been presented with a memento. In a small unmarked Fiat with a blue flashing light on top, "Clouseau" escorted our minibus out of Paris.

CHAPTER 58

Stranger Than Fiction

I had been becoming hypermanic in 2000 and was driving south towards Dover. I had decided to travel to Paris to persuade David Shayler to make a surprise return to England when the authorities were not expecting him. I intended to catch the ferry, and then the train to Paris. But late into the night I lost control of my car and it veered diagonally off the left hand side of the road and careered about 100 metres down an embankment off the motorway. As it was late at night, nobody witnessed the accident. Although the car was written-off later by insurers, I was completely unhurt and escaped through the electric sliding sunroof. I climbed back up the embankment onto the side of the motorway and tried to flag down passing vehicles. But the only vehicles on the motorway at that time of night were heavy lorries on their way to Dover. I walked several hundred yards before I spotted a grey juggernaut parked under a flyover in the hard shoulder. I knocked on the cab door and was invited to get in on the right hand side by the driver. The lorry was a foreign one, with no markings, except for a crown symbol on the doors. I tried to talk to the driver but we simply did not speak each other's language. I pointed to his mobile phone and repeated the word "police" several times. At that moment, a curtain behind the driver's head was wrenched aside and a woman behind the curtain started screaming at the driver in what sounded like Russian. The driver immediately jumped down from his cab, raced around his lorry, and yanked me out of the very high passenger seat by my boots. I was hanging on to the grab handle on the top of the lorry by my hand, but eventually lost my grip. I couldn't break my fall as I hit the road and I heard and felt my spine crack with the impact and screamed in agony. The driver then dragged me around the vehicle, dumped me at the side of the road and then drove off in great haste.

Eventually, and in enormous pain, I managed to catch my breath and get to my feet and look around. I spotted a Holiday Inn sign on the other side of the motorway and I slowly, and very painfully, climbed up the embankment and crossed the flyover. The police were called, and after an initial statement and a breathalyser, I was taken to the hospital in Ashford. My back was checked by the doctor, simply by running her fingers up my spine and, despite my protestations that I had heard a crack, no X-rays were taken. I was told that because I could walk there was no injury to my spine. I was discharged without treatment. The police found my car and retrieved my belongings. As I was in Ashford, I caught the next Eurostar train to Paris to complete my "mission". I remember the disgusted looks I got from some of the Eurostar staff as I sat there dishevelled and dirty after my ordeal in a first class seat. I bought myself a small bottle of champagne and toasted my own good health. I got to Paris and, eventually, to my hotel. As the day progressed, the pain in my back got more severe so that I could no longer bear it and an ambulance took me to a hospital near the Gare du Nord, where I paid for X-rays. These revealed that I had a compound and crushed wedge fracture to my 11th thoracic vertebrae. The pain and shock of the episode and the anger I felt combined to make me high. I managed to make contact with David and Annie and they assisted me as I was taken through a series of French mental hospitals and eventually returned to England. These days I suffer continuous back pain that is focused in my kidneys.

CHAPTER 59

Mohamed Al Fayed & One Left Glove

I wrote a tongue in cheek letter to Mohamed Al Fayed. I told him that, as I only have one arm, I objected to buying a pair of gloves and that as Harrods have a reputation for selling anything from "a pin to an elephant", I was wondering if they would sell me just one left glove. I got a letter back from Mr Fayed offering to make me a tailor-made leather and cashmere glove for the princely sum of £75.

Harrods Glove – Photo with
kind permission of the Evening Gazette, Middlesborough

Harrods measured my hand and instructed Dents, the gents' "accessories" manufacturers, to make me the leather glove. When I received the "garment", I brought it to the attention of the media with the slogan "It cost me an arm and a leg". I sent the substantial press cuttings to Mr Al Fayed and he agreed to meet me to shake my gloved hand. I met with him on a few occasions.

Meeting Mohamed Al Fayed – Photo Keith Whincup

He was a very genuine man who deeply believes that there was more to the death of his son Dodi and Princess Diana than meets the eye. He was also employing David Shayler to write for his magazine "PUNCH", and I had meetings with Mr Al Fayed and his representatives to discuss increasing David's payment while he was still in exile in France.

CHAPTER 60

Doing The Kelly Walk

Football Crazy Logo – designed by Chris Joseph

Finally I come to the love of my life. With the exception of my family and friends, I love my football team, Middlesbrough Football Club, above all else. I have been a "Boro" supporter ever since my father took me to see them as a child. Some people believe that manic depressive psychosis is hereditary, whilst other believe it is brought about by life events. I have a theory that my mood swings could be attributed to the trials and tribulations of being a Boro supporter. I have spent thousands of pounds over the years following my team and travelled many thousands of miles and finally witnessed them picking up their first trophy after 128 years. Boro won the Carling Cup on February 29th 2004. It was the first piece of domestic silverware they have ever won in the history of the club.

Trust the Boro to give their supporters a date they can only commemorate every four years! In 1999, I was listening to the radio in my car when I heard a report that Juninho, the diminutive World Cup winning Brazilian midfield footballer who was arguably the best footballer that Middlesbrough ever had, was returning to Middlesbrough to play for us once again. The former Chief Executive of the Football Association, Graham Kelly, was being interviewed about his reaction to the prospective return of the "little man"; he was full of glowing praise and quipped, "If he returns, I would walk up to Middlesbrough to see Juninho play". Shortly afterwards Juninho came back to Middlesbrough, I contacted a reporter friend of mine, Angus Hoy, and he got me a contact number for Graham Kelly. I rang Graham and reminded him of his comments on the radio. I told him that if he was a man of his word he would make good his promise, and walk the 184 miles from his home in Peterborough up to Teesside to see Juninho play. Graham was quick to agree to the high profile stunt, and we both agreed that we should make it a sponsored walk, raising money for mental health charities.

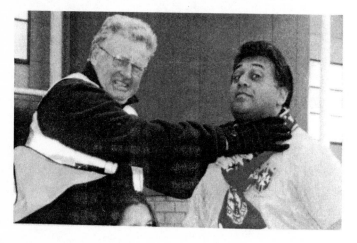

Graham Kelly at full throttle – Photo with kind permission of the Evening Gazette, Middlesbrough

Graham did the walk in November 1999, walking the whole distance over a week and stopping to give interviews to the media about mental health issues and the purpose of his walk. As he arrived on the outskirts of Middlesbrough, he was joined by a merry throng of supporters carrying colourful plastic collection buckets.

Mike J Carr, Mayor of Middlesbrough helps with the collection. – Photo with kind permission of the Evening Gazette, Middlesbrough

The Mayor of Middlesbrough, Michael J. Carr, who was dressed in full garb and chains, walked the last ten miles with Graham and the Boro faithful. At the Riverside Stadium, Graham did a final lap of the pitch and announced to the crowd that we had raised £20,000. Not bad for a daft idea.

CHAPTER 61

Conclusion

Every person experiences joy and pain, both physical and mental, to a greater or lesser degree, and I believe that an individual can only truly empathise with the happiness or suffering of another if they have experienced it for themselves. I have tried to describe my pain and make some sense out of my madness. But hopefully I will bring hope to whoever reads these "manicdotes" and inspire them to laugh through the adversity and cope with whatever life throws at them. I have just reached my fiftieth year but I have experienced much and I will, no doubt, have much more joy and sadness to come. I am a great believer in the axiom "no pain, no gain". I do not regret the negative moments, as they have contributed to what I am. I am the totality of my life's experiences and what I have been taught. I enjoy laughing with my friends but I am able to identify with their pain and hopefully help them through it. Although I am no longer a practising Catholic, my awareness of my "social conscience" burns as fervently as ever. In this book I have bared my chest to ridicule and opened myself up to criticism. I hope my candid descriptions of pain, both physical and mental, serve to de-stigmatise subjects that are taboo. I am not a celebrity and have never broken a metatarsal playing football, but I am infamous with my family and friends. If my experiences help in the slightest then I have achieved something. Overcoming life's obstacles with a degree of lateral thinking, wit, and insanity – where there's a will there's a way. At the moment I'm certified "sane"; how about you…?